Just The facts101
Textbook Key Facts

Textbook Outlines, Highlights, and Practice Quizzes

Investments: An Introduction

by Herbert B. Mayo, 11st Edition

All "Just the Facts101" Material Written or Prepared by Cram101 Publishing

Title Page

Visit Cram101.com for full Practice Exams

WHY STOP HERE... THERE'S MORE ONLINE

With technology and experience, we've developed tools that make studying easier and efficient. Like this Cram101 textbook notebook, Cram101.com offers you the highlights from every chapter of your actual textbook. However, unlike this notebook, Cram101.com gives you practice tests for each of the chapters. You also get access to in-depth reference material for writing essays and papers.

By purchasing this book, you get 50% off the normal subscription free!. Just enter the promotional code **'DK73DW22362'** on the Cram101.com registration screen.

CRAM101.COM FEATURES:

Outlines & Highlights
Just like the ones in this notebook, but with links to additional information.

Integrated Note Taking
Add your class notes to the Cram101 notes, print them and maximize your study time.

Problem Solving
Step-by-step walk throughs for math, stats and other disciplines.

Practice Exams
Five different test taking formats for every chapter.

Easy Access
Study any of your books, on any computer, anywhere.

Unlimited Textbooks
All the features above for virtually all your textbooks, just add them to your account at no additional cost.

Be sure to use the promo code above when registering on Cram101.com to get 50% off your membership fees.

Visit Cram101.com for full Practice Exams

STUDYING MADE EASY

This Cram101 notebook is designed to make studying easier and increase your comprehension of the textbook material. Instead of starting with a blank notebook and trying to write down everything discussed in class lectures, you can use this Cram101 textbook notebook and annotate your notes along with the lecture.

Our goal is to give you the best tools for success.

For a supreme understanding of the course, pair your notebook with our online tools. Should you decide you prefer Cram101.com as your study tool,

we'd like to offer you a trade...

Our Trade In program is a simple way for us to keep our promise and provide you the best studying tools, regardless of where you purchased your Cram101 textbook notebook. As long as your notebook is in *Like New Condition**, you can send it back to us and we will immediately give you a Cram101.com account free for 120 days!

Let The *Trade In* Begin!

THREE SIMPLE STEPS TO TRADE:

1. Go to www.cram101.com/tradein and fill out the packing slip information.
2. Submit and print the packing slip and mail it in with your Cram101 textbook notebook.
3. Activate your account after you receive your email confirmation.

* Books must be returned in *Like New Condition*, meaning there is no damage to the book including, but not limited to; ripped or torn pages, markings or writing on pages, or folded / creased pages. Upon receiving the book, Cram101 will inspect it and reserves the right to terminate your free Cram101.com account and return your textbook notebook at the owners expense.

Visit Cram101.com for full Practice Exams

Cram101 Learning System

"Just the Facts101" is a Cram101 publication and tool designed to give you all the facts from your textbooks. Visit Cram101.com for the full practice test for each of your chapters for virtually any of your textbooks.

Cram101 has built custom study tools specific to your textbook. We provide all of the factual testable information and unlike traditional study guides, we will never send you back to your textbook for more information.

YOU WILL NEVER HAVE TO HIGHLIGHT A BOOK AGAIN!

Cram101 StudyGuides

All of the information in this StudyGuide is written specifically for your textbook. We include the key terms, places, people, and concepts... the information you can expect on your next exam!

Want to take a practice test?

Throughout each chapter of this StudyGuide you will find links to cram101.com where you can select specific chapters to take a complete test on, or you can subscribe and get practice tests for up to 12 of your textbooks, along with other exclusive cram101.com tools like problem solving labs and reference libraries.

Cram101.com

Only cram101.com gives you the outlines, highlights, and PRACTICE TESTS specific to your textbook. Cram101.com is an online application where you'll discover study tools designed to make the most of your limited study time.

By purchasing this book, you get 50% off the normal monthly subscription fee!. Just enter the promotional code **'DK73DW22362'** on the Cram101.com registration screen.

www.Cram101.com

Copyright © 2013 by Cram101, Inc. All rights reserved.
"Just the FACTS101"®, "Cram101"® and "Never Highlight a Book Again!"® are registered trademarks of Cram101, Inc.
ISBN(s): 9781490242408. PUBE-2.201389

Visit Cram101.com for full Practice Exams

facts101

Investments: An Introduction
Herbert B. Mayo, 11st

CONTENTS

1. An Introduction to Investments 5
2. Securities Markets 11
3. The Time Value of Money 21
4. Financial Planning, Taxation, and the Efficiency of Financial Markets 26
5. Risk and Portfolio Management 33
6. Investment Companies: Mutual Funds 45
7. Closed-end Investment Companies, Real Estate Investment Trusts 55
8. Stock 62
9. The Valuation of Common Stock 74
10. Investment Returns and Aggregate Measures of Stock Markets 82
11. The Macroeconomic Environment for Investment Decisions 89
12. Behavioral Finance and Technical Analysis 98
13. The Bond Market 105
14. The Valuation of Fixed-Income Securities 117
15. Government Securities 124
16. Convertible Bonds and Convertible Preferred Stock 132
17. An Introduction to Options 137
18. Option Valuation and Strategies 143
19. Commodity and Financial Futures 149
20. Financial Planning and Investing in an Efficient Market Context 157

Visit Cram101.com for full Practice Exams

1. An Introduction to Investments

CHAPTER OUTLINE: KEY TERMS, PEOPLE, PLACES, CONCEPTS

	P3M3
	Savings account
	Primary market
	Secondary market
	Valuation
	Capital gain
	Rate of return
	Speculation
	Asset allocation
	Diversification
	Certified Financial Planner
	Behavioral Finance

CHAPTER HIGHLIGHTS & NOTES: KEY TERMS, PEOPLE, PLACES, CONCEPTS

P3M3	P3M3, Programme and Project Management Maturity Model is a reference guide for structured best practice. It breaks down the broad disciplines of portfolio, programme and project management into a hierarchy of Key Process Areas (KPAs). The hierarchical approach enables organisations to assess their current capability and then plot a roadmap for improvement prioritised by those KPAs which will make the biggest impact on performance.
Savings account	Saving accounts are accounts maintained by retail financial institutions that pay interest but cannot be used directly as money in the narrow sense of a medium of exchange (for example, by writing a cheque). These accounts let customers set aside a portion of their liquid assets while earning a monetary return.

Visit Cram101.com for full Practice Exams

1. An Introduction to Investments

CHAPTER HIGHLIGHTS & NOTES: KEY TERMS, PEOPLE, PLACES, CONCEPTS

Primary market	The primary market is that part of the capital markets that deals with the issuance of new securities. Companies, governments or public sector institutions can obtain bonds through the sale of a new stock or bond issue. This is typically done through a syndicate of securities dealers.
Secondary market	The secondary market, is the financial market in which previously issued financial instruments such as stock, bonds, options, and futures are bought and sold. Another frequent usage of 'secondary market' is to refer to loans which are sold by a mortgage bank to investors such as Fannie Mae and Freddie Mac.
	The term 'secondary market' is also used to refer to the market for any used goods or assets, or an alternative use for an existing product or asset where the customer base is the second market (for example, corn has been traditionally used primarily for food production and feedstock, but a 'second' or 'third' market has developed for use in ethanol production).
Valuation	In finance, valuation is the process of estimating what something is worth. Items that are usually valued are a financial asset or liability. Valuations can be done on assets (for example, investments in marketable securities such as stocks, options, business enterprises, or intangible assets such as patents and trademarks) or on liabilities (e.g., bonds issued by a company).
Capital gain	A capital gain is a profit that results from a disposition of a capital asset, such as stock, bond or real estate, where the amount realized on the disposition exceeds the purchase price. The gain is the difference between a higher selling price and a lower purchase price. Conversely, a capital loss arises if the proceeds from the sale of a capital asset are less than the purchase price.
Rate of return	In finance, rate of return also known as return on investment (ROI), rate of profit or sometimes just return, is the ratio of money gained or lost (whether realized or unrealized) on an investment relative to the amount of money invested. The amount of money gained or lost may be referred to as interest, profit/loss, gain/loss, or net income/loss. The money invested may be referred to as the asset, capital, principal, or the cost basis of the investment.
Speculation	Speculation is a financial action that does not promise safety of capital investment along with the return on the principal sum. A person or entity that engages in speculation is known as a Speculator. Speculation typically involves the lending of money for the purchase of assets, equity or debt but in a manner that has not been given thorough analysis or is deemed to have low margin of safety or a significant risk of the loss of the principal investment.
Asset allocation	Asset allocation is an investment strategy that attempts to balance risk versus reward by adjusting the percentage of each asset in an investment portfolio according to the investors risk tolerance, goals and investment time frame. Description
	Many financial experts say that asset allocation is an important factor in determining returns for an investment portfolio.

1. An Introduction to Investments

CHAPTER HIGHLIGHTS & NOTES: KEY TERMS, PEOPLE, PLACES, CONCEPTS

Diversification	Diversification is a form of corporate strategy for a company. It seeks to increase profitability through greater sales volume obtained from new products and new markets. Diversification can occur either at the business unit level or at the corporate level.
Certified Financial Planner	The Certified Financial Planner designation is a professional certification mark for financial planners conferred by the Certified Financial Planner Board of Standards (Certified Financial Planner Board) in the United States, Financial Planning Standards Council in Canada and 22 other organizations affiliated with Financial Planning Standards Board (FPSB), the international owner of the Certified Financial Planner mark outside of the United States. To receive authorization to use the designation, the candidate must meet education, examination, experience and ethics requirements, and pay an ongoing certification fee. The information relates specifically to Certified Financial Planner certification in the United States.
Behavioral Finance	Behavioral economics and the related field, behavioral finance, study the effects of social, cognitive, and emotional factors on the economic decisions of individuals and institutions and the consequences for market prices, returns, and the resource allocation. The fields are primarily concerned with the bounds of rationality of economic agents. Behavioral models typically integrate insights from psychology with neo-classical economic theory.

CHAPTER QUIZ: KEY TERMS, PEOPLE, PLACES, CONCEPTS

1. In finance, _____ also known as return on investment (ROI), rate of profit or sometimes just return, is the ratio of money gained or lost (whether realized or unrealized) on an investment relative to the amount of money invested. The amount of money gained or lost may be referred to as interest, profit/loss, gain/loss, or net income/loss. The money invested may be referred to as the asset, capital, principal, or the cost basis of the investment.

    a. Rate of return
    b. Rolling
    c. Same-day affirmation
    d. Tax audit representation

2. . _____, Programme and Project Management Maturity Model is a reference guide for structured best practice. It breaks down the broad disciplines of portfolio, programme and project management into a hierarchy of Key Process Areas (KPAs). The hierarchical approach enables organisations to assess their current capability and then plot a roadmap for improvement prioritised by those KPAs which will make the biggest impact on performance.

    a. Phased implementation

1. An Introduction to Investments

CHAPTER QUIZ: KEY TERMS, PEOPLE, PLACES, CONCEPTS

   b. Phase-gate model
   c. P3M3
   d. Pmhub

3. Saving accounts are accounts maintained by retail financial institutions that pay interest but cannot be used directly as money in the narrow sense of a medium of exchange (for example, by writing a cheque). These accounts let customers set aside a portion of their liquid assets while earning a monetary return. For the bank, money in a _____ may not be callable immediately and in some jurisdictions, does not incur a reserve requirement, freeing up cash from the bank's vault to be lent out with interest.

   a. Service release premium
   b. Savings account
   c. Single Supervisory Mechanism
   d. Soft probe

4. The _____ is that part of the capital markets that deals with the issuance of new securities. Companies, governments or public sector institutions can obtain bonds through the sale of a new stock or bond issue. This is typically done through a syndicate of securities dealers.

   a. price-weighted
   b. granularity
   c. Primary market
   d. Soft probe

5. _____ is an investment strategy that attempts to balance risk versus reward by adjusting the percentage of each asset in an investment portfolio according to the investors risk tolerance, goals and investment time frame. Description

   Many financial experts say that _____ is an important factor in determining returns for an investment portfolio. _____ is based on the principle that different assets perform differently in different market and economic conditions.

   a. Asset Liquidation Marketing Integration Within Asset Management Framework
   b. Asset location
   c. Asset allocation
   d. Eco-investing

Visit Cram101.com for full Practice Exams

ANSWER KEY
1. An Introduction to Investments

1. a
2. c
3. b
4. c
5. c

You can take the complete Chapter Practice Test

for 1. An Introduction to Investments
on all key terms, persons, places, and concepts.

Online 99 Cents

http://www.epub2174.13.22362.1.cram101.com/

Use www.Cram101.com for all your study needs

including Cram101's online interactive problem solving labs in

chemistry, statistics, mathematics, and more.

Visit Cram101.com for full Practice Exams

2. Securities Markets

CHAPTER OUTLINE: KEY TERMS, PEOPLE, PLACES, CONCEPTS

- Market maker
- Financial Industry Regulatory Authority
- Primary market
- Secondary market
- Round lot
- Block trade
- Instinet
- Third market
- Buy side
- OTC Markets Group
- Brokerage firm
- Bullish
- Long position
- CUSIP
- Margin
- Settlement date
- Common stock
- Margin account
- Book entry
- Short sale
- American depositary receipt

Visit Cram101.com for full Practice Exams

2. Securities Markets
CHAPTER OUTLINE: KEY TERMS, PEOPLE, PLACES, CONCEPTS

- Sarbanes-Oxley Act
- Investment bank
- Public Company Accounting Oversight Board
- Federal Deposit Insurance Corporation
- Private placement
- Concept note
- Merchant bank
- Underwriting
- Firm commitment
- Shelf registration

CHAPTER HIGHLIGHTS & NOTES: KEY TERMS, PEOPLE, PLACES, CONCEPTS

Market maker	A market maker is a company, or an individual, that quotes both a buy and a sell price in a financial instrument or commodity held in inventory, hoping to make a profit on the bid-offer spread, or turn. In currency exchange Most foreign exchange trading firms are market makers and so are many banks. The market maker sells to and buys from its clients and is compensated by means of price differentials for the service of providing liquidity, reducing transaction costs and facilitating trade.
Financial Industry Regulatory Authority	In the United States, the Financial Industry Regulatory Authority, Inc., or FINRA, is a private corporation that acts as a self-regulatory organization (SRO). FINRA is the successor to the National Association of Securities Dealers, Inc. (NASD).
Primary market	The primary market is that part of the capital markets that deals with the issuance of new securities. Companies, governments or public sector institutions can obtain bonds through the sale of a new stock or bond issue.

Visit Cram101.com for full Practice Exams

2. Securities Markets

CHAPTER HIGHLIGHTS & NOTES: KEY TERMS, PEOPLE, PLACES, CONCEPTS

Secondary market	The secondary market, is the financial market in which previously issued financial instruments such as stock, bonds, options, and futures are bought and sold. Another frequent usage of 'secondary market' is to refer to loans which are sold by a mortgage bank to investors such as Fannie Mae and Freddie Mac. The term 'secondary market' is also used to refer to the market for any used goods or assets, or an alternative use for an existing product or asset where the customer base is the second market (for example, corn has been traditionally used primarily for food production and feedstock, but a 'second' or 'third' market has developed for use in ethanol production).
Round lot	A round lot is a normal unit of trading of a security, which is usually 100 shares of stock. Any quantity less than this normal unit is referred to as an odd lot.
Block trade	A block trade is a permissible, noncompetitive, privately negotiated transaction either at or exceeding an exchange determined minimum threshold quantity of shares, which is executed apart and away from the open outcry or electronic markets. In the United States and Canada a block trade is usually at least 10,000 shares of a stock or $200,000 of bonds but in practice significantly larger. For instance, a hedge fund holds a large position in Company X and would like to sell it completely.
Instinet	Instinet is an institutional, agency-only broker that also serves as the independent equity trading arm of its parent, Nomura. It executes trades for roughly 1,500 'buyside' clients such as asset management firms, hedge funds, insurance companies, mutual funds and pension funds. Headquartered in New York and with offices in twelve other cities around the world, the company provides sales trading services and trading technologies such as the Newport EMS, algorithms, trade cost analytics, commission management, independent research and dark pools of liquidity.
Third market	Third market in finance, refers to the trading of exchange-listed securities in the over-the-counter (OTC) market. These trades allow institutional investors to trade blocks of securities directly, rather than through an exchange, providing liquidity and anonymity to buyers Third market trading was pioneered in the 1960s by firms such as Jefferies & Company although today there are a number of brokerage firms focused on third market trading, and more recently dark pools of liquidity.
Buy side	Buy-side is a term used in investment banking to refer to advising institutions concerned with buying investment services. Private equity funds, mutual funds, life insurance companies, unit trusts, hedge funds, and pension funds are the most common types of buy side entities.

Visit Cram101.com for full Practice Exams

2. Securities Markets

CHAPTER HIGHLIGHTS & NOTES: KEY TERMS, PEOPLE, PLACES, CONCEPTS

OTC Markets Group	OTC Markets Group, Inc. (OTCQX: OTCM), headquartered in New York City, operates a financial marketplace platform providing price and liquidity information for almost 10,000 OTC securities. OTC-traded securities are organized into three marketplaces to inform investors of opportunities and risks: OTCQX, OTCQB and OTC Pink.
Brokerage firm	A brokerage firm, is a financial institution that facilitates the buying and selling of financial securities between a buyer and a seller. Brokerage firms serve a clientele of investors who trade public stocks and other securities, usually through the firm's agent stockbrokers. A traditional, or 'full service', brokerage firm usually undertakes more than simply carrying out a stock or bond trade.
Bullish	Market sentiment is the general prevailing attitude of investors as to anticipated price development in a market. This attitude is the accumulation of a variety of fundamental and technical factors, including price history, economic reports, seasonal factors, and national and world events. For example, if investors expect upward price movement in the stock market, the sentiment is said to be bullish.
Long position	In finance, a long position in a security, such as a stock or a bond, or equivalently to be long in a security, means the holder of the position owns the security and will profit if the price of the security goes up. Going long is the more conventional practice of investing and is contrasted with going short. An options investor goes long on the underlying instrument by buying call options or writing put options on it.
CUSIP	A CUSIP is a 9-character alphanumeric code which identifies a North American financial security for the purposes of facilitating clearing and settlement of trades. The CUSIP distribution system is owned by the American Bankers Association, and is operated by Standard & Poor's. The CUSIP Service Bureau acts as the National numbering agency (NNA) for North America, and the CUSIP serves as the National Securities Identification Number for products issued from both the United States and Canada.
Margin	In finance, a margin is collateral that the holder of a financial instrument has to deposit to cover some or all of the credit risk of their counterparty (most often their broker or an exchange). This risk can arise if the holder has done any of the following:•borrowed cash from the counterparty to buy financial instruments,•sold financial instruments short, or•entered into a derivative contract. The collateral can be in the form of cash or securities, and it is deposited in a margin account. On United States futures exchanges, 'margin' was formerly called performance bond.
Settlement date	Settlement Date is a securities industry term describing the date on which a trade (bonds, equities, foreign exchange, commodities, etc). settles.

Visit Cram101.com for full Practice Exams

2. Securities Markets

CHAPTER HIGHLIGHTS & NOTES: KEY TERMS, PEOPLE, PLACES, CONCEPTS

Common stock	Common stock is a form of corporate equity ownership, a type of security. The terms 'voting share' or 'ordinary share' are also used in other parts of the world; common stock being primarily used in the United States. It is called 'common' to distinguish it from preferred stock.
Margin account	In finance, a margin is collateral that the holder of a financial instrument has to deposit to cover some or all of the credit risk of their counterparty (most often their broker or an exchange). This risk can arise if the holder has done any of the following:•Borrowed cash from the counterparty to buy financial instruments,•Sold financial instruments short, or•Entered into a derivative contract The collateral can be in the form of cash or securities, and it is deposited in a margin account. On United States futures exchanges, margins were formerly called performance bonds.
Book entry	Book entry is a system of tracking ownership of securities where no certificate is given to investors. In the case of book-entry-only (BEO) issues, while investors do not receive certificates, a custodian holds one or more global certificates. Dematerialized securities, in contrast are ones in which no certificates exist, instead, the security issuer or its agent keeps records, usually electronically, of who holds outstanding securities.
Short sale	A short sale is a sale of real estate in which the sale proceeds fall short of the balance owed on the property's loan. It often occurs when a borrower cannot pay the mortgage loan on their property, but the lender decides that selling the property at a moderate loss is better than pressing the borrower. Both parties consent to the short sale process, because it allows them to avoid foreclosure, which involves hefty fees for the bank and poorer credit report outcomes for the borrowers.
American depositary receipt	An American depositary receipt is a negotiable security that represents securities of a non-US company that trade in the US financial markets. Securities of a foreign company that are represented by an American depositary receipt are called American depositary shares (ADSs). Shares of many non-US companies trade on US stock exchanges through American depositary receipts.
Sarbanes-Oxley Act	The Sarbanes-Oxley Act of 2002 (Pub.L. 107-204, 116 Stat. 745, enacted July 29, 2002), also known as the 'Public Company Accounting Reform and Investor Protection Act' (in the Senate) and 'Corporate and Auditing Accountability and Responsibility Act' (in the House) and more commonly called Sarbanes-Oxley, Sarbox or SOX, is a United States federal law that set new or enhanced standards for all U.S. public company boards, management and public accounting firms. ponsors U.S. Senator Paul Sarbanes (D-MD) and U.S. Representative Michael G. Oxley (R-OH). As a result of SOX, top management must now individually certify the accuracy of financial information.

Visit Cram101.com for full Practice Exams

2. Securities Markets

CHAPTER HIGHLIGHTS & NOTES: KEY TERMS, PEOPLE, PLACES, CONCEPTS

Investment bank	An investment bank is a financial institution that assists individuals, corporations and governments in raising capital by underwriting and/or acting as the client's agent in the issuance of securities. An investment bank may also assist companies involved in mergers and acquisitions, and provide ancillary services such as market making, trading of derivatives, fixed income instruments, foreign exchange, commodities, and equity securities. Unlike commercial banks and retail banks, investment banks do not take deposits.
Public Company Accounting Oversight Board	The Public Company Accounting Oversight Board is a private-sector, non-profit corporation created by the Sarbanes-Oxley Act, a 2002 United States federal law, to oversee the auditors of public companies. Its stated purpose is to 'protect the interests of investors and further the public interest in the preparation of informative, fair, and independent audit reports'. Although a private entity, the Public Company Accounting Oversight Board has many government-like regulatory functions, making it in some ways similar to the private 'self-regulatory organizations' (SROs) which regulate stock markets, broker-dealers, etc.
Federal Deposit Insurance Corporation	The Federal Deposit Insurance Corporation is a United States government corporation created by the Glass-Steagall Act of 1933. It provides deposit insurance, which guarantees the safety of deposits in member banks, up to $250,000 per depositor per bank as of January 2012. As of November 18, 2010 (2010 -11-18), the federal\ deposit\ insurance\ corporation insured deposits at 7,723 institutions. The federal\ deposit\ insurance\ corporation also examines and supervises certain financial institutions for safety and soundness, performs certain consumer-protection functions, and manages banks in receiverships (failed banks). Insured institutions are required to place signs at their place of business stating that 'deposits are backed by the full faith and credit of the United States Government.' Since the start of federal\ deposit\ insurance\ corporation insurance on January 1, 1934, no depositor has lost any insured funds as a result of a failure.
Private placement	Private placement is a funding round of securities which are sold not through a public offering, but rather through a private offering, mostly to a small number of chosen investors. 'Private placement' usually refers to non-public offering of shares in a public company (since, of course, any offering of shares in a private company is and can only be a private offering). PIPE (private investment in public equity) deals are one type of private placement.
Concept note	A concept note, is a preliminary description of the ideas behind a project. Businesses and nonprofit organizations use them to help test and refine concepts and to communicate about the project with potential partners and donors. In education, concept notes may be used by students embarking on research to gather and present preliminary ideas.

Visit Cram101.com for full Practice Exams

2. Securities Markets

CHAPTER HIGHLIGHTS & NOTES: KEY TERMS, PEOPLE, PLACES, CONCEPTS

Merchant bank	A merchant bank is a financial institution which provides capital to companies in the form of share ownership instead of loans. A merchant bank also provides advisory on corporate matters to the firms they lend to. In the United Kingdom, the term 'merchant bank' refers to an investment bank.
Underwriting	Underwriting refers to the process that a large financial service provider (bank, insurer, investment house) uses to assess the eligibility of a customer to receive their products (equity capital, insurance, mortgage, or credit). The name derives from the Lloyd's of London insurance market. Financial bankers, who would accept some of the risk on a given venture (historically a sea voyage with associated risks of shipwreck) in exchange for a premium, would literally write their names under the risk information that was written on a Lloyd's slip created for this purpose.
Firm commitment	In investment banking, an underwriting contract is a contract between an underwriter and an issuer of securities. The following types of underwriting contracts are most common:•In the firm commitment contract the underwriter guarantees the sale of the issued stock at the agreed-upon price. For the issuer, it is the safest but the most expensive type of the contracts, since the underwriter takes the risk of sale.•In the best efforts contract the underwriter agrees to sell as many shares as possible at the agreed-upon price.
Shelf registration	Shelf registration is a process authorized by the U.S. Securities and Exchange Commission under Rule 415 that allows a single registration document to be filed by a company that permits the issuance of multiple securities. Form S-3 issuers may use shelf-registration to register securities that will be offered on an immediate, continuous, or even on a delayed basis. Other special types of securities, such as those used in a business combination, Mortgage backed securities, and those of a closed-end fund.

CHAPTER QUIZ: KEY TERMS, PEOPLE, PLACES, CONCEPTS

1. . Buy-side is a term used in investment banking to refer to advising institutions concerned with buying investment services. Private equity funds, mutual funds, life insurance companies, unit trusts, hedge funds, and pension funds are the most common types of _____ entities.

    In sales & trading, the split between the _____ and sell side should be viewed from the perspective of securities exchange services.

    a. Cable
    b. Capital structure substitution theory
    c. Buy side

Visit Cram101.com for full Practice Exams

2. Securities Markets

CHAPTER QUIZ: KEY TERMS, PEOPLE, PLACES, CONCEPTS

2. A _____ is a sale of real estate in which the sale proceeds fall short of the balance owed on the property's loan. It often occurs when a borrower cannot pay the mortgage loan on their property, but the lender decides that selling the property at a moderate loss is better than pressing the borrower. Both parties consent to the _____ process, because it allows them to avoid foreclosure, which involves hefty fees for the bank and poorer credit report outcomes for the borrowers.

   a. Short sale
   b. Convertible security
   c. Direct holding system
   d. Distressed lending

3. The _____, is the financial market in which previously issued financial instruments such as stock, bonds, options, and futures are bought and sold. Another frequent usage of '_____' is to refer to loans which are sold by a mortgage bank to investors such as Fannie Mae and Freddie Mac.

   The term '_____' is also used to refer to the market for any used goods or assets, or an alternative use for an existing product or asset where the customer base is the second market (for example, corn has been traditionally used primarily for food production and feedstock, but a 'second' or 'third' market has developed for use in ethanol production).

   a. Short
   b. Short and distort
   c. Securities Industry and Financial Markets Association
   d. Secondary market

4. In investment banking, an underwriting contract is a contract between an underwriter and an issuer of securities.

   The following types of underwriting contracts are most common:•In the _____ contract the underwriter guarantees the sale of the issued stock at the agreed-upon price. For the issuer, it is the safest but the most expensive type of the contracts, since the underwriter takes the risk of sale.•In the best efforts contract the underwriter agrees to sell as many shares as possible at the agreed-upon price.

   a. Breach of contract
   b. Firm commitment
   c. Jimmy Carter
   d. Utilization management

5. . A _____ is a company, or an individual, that quotes both a buy and a sell price in a financial instrument or commodity held in inventory, hoping to make a profit on the bid-offer spread, or turn. In currency exchange

   Most foreign exchange trading firms are _____s and so are many banks. The _____ sells to and buys from its clients and is compensated by means of price differentials for the service of providing liquidity, reducing transaction costs and facilitating trade.

   a. Market portfolio

2. Securities Markets

CHAPTER QUIZ: KEY TERMS, PEOPLE, PLACES, CONCEPTS

b. Market profile
c. Market saturation
d. Market maker

ANSWER KEY
2. Securities Markets

1. c
2. a
3. d
4. b
5. d

You can take the complete Chapter Practice Test

for 2. Securities Markets
on all key terms, persons, places, and concepts.

Online 99 Cents

http://www.epub2174.13.22362.2.cram101.com/

Use www.Cram101.com for all your study needs

including Cram101's online interactive problem solving labs in

chemistry, statistics, mathematics, and more.

Visit Cram101.com for full Practice Exams

3. The Time Value of Money

CHAPTER OUTLINE: KEY TERMS, PEOPLE, PLACES, CONCEPTS

- Discounting
- Annuity
- Future value
- Present value
- Valuation
- Yield to maturity

CHAPTER HIGHLIGHTS & NOTES: KEY TERMS, PEOPLE, PLACES, CONCEPTS

Discounting	Discounting is a financial mechanism in which a debtor obtains the right to delay payments to a creditor, for a defined period of time, in exchange for a charge or fee. Essentially, the party that owes money in the present purchases the right to delay the payment until some future date. The discount, or charge, is simply the difference between the original amount owed in the present and the amount that has to be paid in the future to settle the debt.
Annuity	The term annuity is used in finance theory, this is to refer to any terminating stream of fixed payments over a specified period of time. This usage is most commonly seen in discussions of finance, usually in connection with the valuation of the stream of payments, taking into account time value of money, concepts such as interest rate and future value. Examples of annuities are regular deposits to a savings account, monthly home mortgage payments and monthly insurance payments.
Future value	Future value is the value of an asset at a specific date. It measures the nominal future sum of money that a given sum of money is 'worth' at a specified time in the future assuming a certain interest rate, or more generally, rate of return; it is the present value multiplied by the accumulation function. The value does not include corrections for inflation or other factors that affect the true value of money in the future.
Present value	Present value, is the value on a given date of a payment or series of payments made at other times.

Visit Cram101.com for full Practice Exams

3. The Time Value of Money

CHAPTER HIGHLIGHTS & NOTES: KEY TERMS, PEOPLE, PLACES, CONCEPTS

	If the payments are in the future, they are discounted to reflect the time value of money and other factors such as investment risk. If they are in the past, their value is correspondingly enhanced to reflect that those payments have been earning interest in the intervening time.
Valuation	In finance, valuation is the process of estimating what something is worth. Items that are usually valued are a financial asset or liability. Valuations can be done on assets (for example, investments in marketable securities such as stocks, options, business enterprises, or intangible assets such as patents and trademarks) or on liabilities (e.g., bonds issued by a company).
Yield to maturity	The Yield to maturity or redemption yield of a bond or other fixed-interest security, such as gilts, is the internal rate of return (IRR, overall interest rate) earned by an investor who buys the bond today at the market price, assuming that the bond will be held until maturity, and that all coupon and principal payments will be made on schedule. Contrary to popular belief, including concepts often cited in advanced financial literature, Yield to maturity does NOT depend upon a reinvestment of coupon payments. Yield to maturity, rather, is simply the discount rate at which the sum of all future cash flows from the bond (coupons and principal) is equal to the price of the bond.

CHAPTER QUIZ: KEY TERMS, PEOPLE, PLACES, CONCEPTS

1. _____ is a financial mechanism in which a debtor obtains the right to delay payments to a creditor, for a defined period of time, in exchange for a charge or fee. Essentially, the party that owes money in the present purchases the right to delay the payment until some future date. The discount, or charge, is simply the difference between the original amount owed in the present and the amount that has to be paid in the future to settle the debt.

   a. Domestic liability dollarization
   b. Down payment
   c. Downside risk
   d. Discounting

2. . The term _____ is used in finance theory, this is to refer to any terminating stream of fixed payments over a specified period of time. This usage is most commonly seen in discussions of finance, usually in connection with the valuation of the stream of payments, taking into account time value of money, concepts such as interest rate and future value.

   Examples of _____(ies) are regular deposits to a savings account, monthly home mortgage payments and monthly insurance payments.

   a. Efficiency Based Absorption Costing

Visit Cram101.com for full Practice Exams

3. The Time Value of Money

CHAPTER QUIZ: KEY TERMS, PEOPLE, PLACES, CONCEPTS

   b. Down payment
   c. Downside risk
   d. Annuity

3. _____ is the value of an asset at a specific date. It measures the nominal future sum of money that a given sum of money is 'worth' at a specified time in the future assuming a certain interest rate, or more generally, rate of return; it is the present value multiplied by the accumulation function. The value does not include corrections for inflation or other factors that affect the true value of money in the future.

   a. Graham number
   b. Heston model
   c. High-frequency trading
   d. Future value

4. The _____ or redemption yield of a bond or other fixed-interest security, such as gilts, is the internal rate of return (IRR, overall interest rate) earned by an investor who buys the bond today at the market price, assuming that the bond will be held until maturity, and that all coupon and principal payments will be made on schedule. Contrary to popular belief, including concepts often cited in advanced financial literature, _____ does NOT depend upon a reinvestment of coupon payments. _____, rather, is simply the discount rate at which the sum of all future cash flows from the bond (coupons and principal) is equal to the price of the bond.

   a. granularity
   b. Virtual bidding
   c. Yield to maturity
   d. Yellow strip

5. In finance, _____ is the process of estimating what something is worth. Items that are usually valued are a financial asset or liability. _____s can be done on assets (for example, investments in marketable securities such as stocks, options, business enterprises, or intangible assets such as patents and trademarks) or on liabilities (e.g., bonds issued by a company).

   a. Valuation
   b. Virtual bidding
   c. Volatility arbitrage
   d. Yellow strip

Visit Cram101.com for full Practice Exams

ANSWER KEY
3. The Time Value of Money

1. d
2. d
3. d
4. c
5. a

You can take the complete Chapter Practice Test

for 3. The Time Value of Money
on all key terms, persons, places, and concepts.

Online 99 Cents

http://www.epub2174.13.22362.3.cram101.com/

Use www.Cram101.com for all your study needs

including Cram101's online interactive problem solving labs in

chemistry, statistics, mathematics, and more.

4. Financial Planning, Taxation, and the Efficiency of Financial Markets

CHAPTER OUTLINE: KEY TERMS, PEOPLE, PLACES, CONCEPTS

- Financial planning
- Mortgage loan
- Asset allocation
- Stock index
- Capital loss
- Wash sale
- Individual retirement accounts
- Annuity
- Price adjustment
- Insider trading
- January effect
- Neglected firm effect
- Stock valuation

Visit Cram101.com for full Practice Exams

4. Financial Planning, Taxation, and the Efficiency of Financial Markets

CHAPTER HIGHLIGHTS & NOTES: KEY TERMS, PEOPLE, PLACES, CONCEPTS

Financial planning	Financial planning is the task of determining how a business will afford to achieve its strategic goals and objectives. Usually, a company creates a Financial Plan immediately after the vision and objectives have been set. The Financial Plan describes each of the activities, resources, equipment and materials that are needed to achieve these objectives, as well as the timeframes involved.
Mortgage loan	A mortgage loan is a loan secured by real property through the use of a mortgage note which evidences the existence of the loan and the encumbrance of that realty through the granting of a mortgage which secures the loan. However, the word mortgage alone, in everyday usage, is most often used to mean mortgage loan. The word mortgage is a French Law term meaning 'death contract', meaning that the pledge ends (dies) when either the obligation is fulfilled or the property is taken through foreclosure.
Asset allocation	Asset allocation is an investment strategy that attempts to balance risk versus reward by adjusting the percentage of each asset in an investment portfolio according to the investors risk tolerance, goals and investment time frame. Description Many financial experts say that asset allocation is an important factor in determining returns for an investment portfolio. Asset allocation is based on the principle that different assets perform differently in different market and economic conditions.
Stock index	A stock index is a method of measuring the value of a section of the stock market. It is computed from the prices of selected stocks (sometimes a weighted average). It is a tool used by investors and financial managers to describe the market, and to compare the return on specific investments.
Capital loss	Capital loss is the difference between a lower selling price and a higher purchase price, resulting in a financial loss for the seller. The IRS states that 'If your capital losses exceed your capital gains, the excess can be deducted on your tax return'. Limits on such deductions apply.
Wash sale	A wash sale is a sale of a security (stock, bonds, options) at a loss and repurchasing the same or substantially identical stock soon afterwards (Internal Revenue Code Sec. 1091). The idea is to make an unrealised loss claimable as a tax deduction, by offsetting against other capital gains in the current or future tax years. The security is repurchased in the hope that it will recover its previous value.
Individual retirement accounts	An Individual Retirement Account is a form of 'individual retirement plan', provided by many financial institutions, that provides tax advantages for retirement savings in the United States. An individual retirement account is a type of 'individual retirement arrangement' as described in IRS Publication 590, Individual Retirement Arrangements .

Visit Cram101.com for full Practice Exams

4. Financial Planning, Taxation, and the Efficiency of Financial Markets

CHAPTER HIGHLIGHTS & NOTES: KEY TERMS, PEOPLE, PLACES, CONCEPTS

Annuity	The term annuity is used in finance theory, this is to refer to any terminating stream of fixed payments over a specified period of time. This usage is most commonly seen in discussions of finance, usually in connection with the valuation of the stream of payments, taking into account time value of money, concepts such as interest rate and future value. Examples of annuities are regular deposits to a savings account, monthly home mortgage payments and monthly insurance payments.
Price adjustment	Price adjustments, also called price protection, occur when a customer buys a product at full price, and then, within a given time frame, that product goes on sale. Retailers will do a 'price adjustment,' refunding the difference between the price the customer paid and the price now available. For example, if a customer buys a TV from Best Buy for $300, and it drops in price by $100, they can go back to the retailer to ask for a price adjustment and get the difference returned to them, often in cash.
Insider trading	Insider trading is the trading of a corporation's stock or other securities (e.g. bonds or stock options) by individuals with potential access to non-public information about the company. In most countries, trading by corporate insiders such as officers, key employees, directors, and large shareholders may be legal, if this trading is done in a way that does not take advantage of non-public information. However, the term is frequently used to refer to a practice in which an insider or a related party trades based on material non-public information obtained during the performance of the insider's duties at the corporation, or otherwise in breach of a fiduciary or other relationship of trust and confidence or where the non-public information was misappropriated from the company.
January effect	The January effect is a calendar-related anomaly in the financial market where financial security prices increase in the month of January. This creates an opportunity for investors to buy stock for lower prices before January and sell them after their value increases. Therefore, the main characteristics of the January Effect are an increase in buying securities before the end of the year for a lower price, and selling them in January to generate profit from the price differences.
Neglected firm effect	The Neglected firm effect is the phenomenon of lesser-known firms producing abnormally high returns on their stocks. The companies that are followed by fewer analysts will earn higher returns on average than companies that are followed by many analysts. The abnormally high return exhibited by neglected firms may be due to the lower liquidity or higher risks associated with the stock.
Stock valuation	In financial markets, stock valuation is the method of calculating theoretical values of companies and their stocks.

4. Financial Planning, Taxation, and the Efficiency of Financial Markets

CHAPTER HIGHLIGHTS & NOTES: KEY TERMS, PEOPLE, PLACES, CONCEPTS

The main use of these methods is to predict future market prices, or more generally, potential market prices, and thus to profit from price movement - stocks that are judged undervalued (with respect to their theoretical value) are bought, while stocks that are judged overvalued are sold, in the expectation that undervalued stocks will, on the whole, rise in value, while overvalued stocks will, on the whole, fall.

In the view of fundamental analysis, stock valuation based on fundamentals aims to give an estimate of their intrinsic value of the stock, based on predictions of the future cash flows and profitability of the business.

CHAPTER QUIZ: KEY TERMS, PEOPLE, PLACES, CONCEPTS

1. _____ is the task of determining how a business will afford to achieve its strategic goals and objectives. Usually, a company creates a Financial Plan immediately after the vision and objectives have been set. The Financial Plan describes each of the activities, resources, equipment and materials that are needed to achieve these objectives, as well as the timeframes involved.

   a. Flexible product development
   b. Float
   c. Front-end loading
   d. Financial planning

2. A _____ is a loan secured by real property through the use of a mortgage note which evidences the existence of the loan and the encumbrance of that realty through the granting of a mortgage which secures the loan. However, the word mortgage alone, in everyday usage, is most often used to mean _____.

   The word mortgage is a French Law term meaning 'death contract', meaning that the pledge ends (dies) when either the obligation is fulfilled or the property is taken through foreclosure.

   a. Balloon payment mortgage
   b. Bank walkaway
   c. Mortgage belt
   d. Mortgage loan

3. . A _____ is a sale of a security (stock, bonds, options) at a loss and repurchasing the same or substantially identical stock soon afterwards (Internal Revenue Code Sec. 1091). The idea is to make an unrealised loss claimable as a tax deduction, by offsetting against other capital gains in the current or future tax years. The security is repurchased in the hope that it will recover its previous value.

Visit Cram101.com for full Practice Exams

4. Financial Planning, Taxation, and the Efficiency of Financial Markets

CHAPTER QUIZ: KEY TERMS, PEOPLE, PLACES, CONCEPTS

a. Wash trade
b. Wealth management
c. WeSeed
d. Wash sale

4. _____ is an investment strategy that attempts to balance risk versus reward by adjusting the percentage of each asset in an investment portfolio according to the investors risk tolerance, goals and investment time frame. Description

    Many financial experts say that _____ is an important factor in determining returns for an investment portfolio. _____ is based on the principle that different assets perform differently in different market and economic conditions.

    a. Asset Liquidation Marketing Integration Within Asset Management Framework
    b. Asset location
    c. Assets under management
    d. Asset allocation

5. The term _____ is used in finance theory, this is to refer to any terminating stream of fixed payments over a specified period of time. This usage is most commonly seen in discussions of finance, usually in connection with the valuation of the stream of payments, taking into account time value of money, concepts such as interest rate and future value.

    Examples of _____(ies) are regular deposits to a savings account, monthly home mortgage payments and monthly insurance payments.

    a. Efficiency Based Absorption Costing
    b. Wealth management
    c. Annuity
    d. Whisper number

ANSWER KEY
4. Financial Planning, Taxation, and the Efficiency of Financial Markets

1. d
2. d
3. d
4. d
5. c

You can take the complete Chapter Practice Test

for 4. Financial Planning, Taxation, and the Efficiency of Financial Markets
on all key terms, persons, places, and concepts.

Online 99 Cents

http://www.epub2174.13.22362.4.cram101.com/

Use www.Cram101.com for all your study needs

including Cram101's online interactive problem solving labs in

chemistry, statistics, mathematics, and more.

5. Risk and Portfolio Management

CHAPTER OUTLINE: KEY TERMS, PEOPLE, PLACES, CONCEPTS

_____ Capital gain

_____ Expected return

_____ Savings account

_____ Holding period return

_____ Systematic risk

_____ Market risk

_____ Deflation

_____ Revaluation

_____ Business risks

_____ Collateral

_____ High-yield bond

_____ Leverage

_____ Diversification

_____ Financial risk

_____ Standard deviation

_____ Semivariance

_____ Coefficient of variation

_____ P3M3

_____ Covariance

_____ Arbitrage pricing theory

_____ Asset allocation

Visit Cram101.com for full Practice Exams

5. Risk and Portfolio Management
CHAPTER OUTLINE: KEY TERMS, PEOPLE, PLACES, CONCEPTS

	Capital asset pricing model
	Efficient frontier
	Indifference curve
	Capital market line
	Security market line
	Coefficient of determination
	Value Line
	Volatility
	Estimation
	Stock index
	American Association of Individual Investors
	Kurtosis

CHAPTER HIGHLIGHTS & NOTES: KEY TERMS, PEOPLE, PLACES, CONCEPTS

Capital gain	A capital gain is a profit that results from a disposition of a capital asset, such as stock, bond or real estate, where the amount realized on the disposition exceeds the purchase price. The gain is the difference between a higher selling price and a lower purchase price. Conversely, a capital loss arises if the proceeds from the sale of a capital asset are less than the purchase price.
Expected return	The expected return is the expected value of a random variable usually representing a gain, i.e. the weighted-average outcome in gambling, probability theory, economics or finance. It is calculated by using the following formula:

5. Risk and Portfolio Management

CHAPTER HIGHLIGHTS & NOTES: KEY TERMS, PEOPLE, PLACES, CONCEPTS

	How do you calculate the average of a probability distribution? As denoted by the above formula, simply take the probability of each possible return outcome and multiply it by the return outcome itself. For example, if you knew a given investment had a 50% chance of earning a 10 return, a 25% chance of earning 20 and a 25% chance of earning -10, the expected return would be equal to 7.5:
	Although this is what you expect the return to be, there is no guarantee that it will be the actual return.
Savings account	Saving accounts are accounts maintained by retail financial institutions that pay interest but cannot be used directly as money in the narrow sense of a medium of exchange (for example, by writing a cheque). These accounts let customers set aside a portion of their liquid assets while earning a monetary return. For the bank, money in a savings account may not be callable immediately and in some jurisdictions, does not incur a reserve requirement, freeing up cash from the bank's vault to be lent out with interest.
Holding period return	In finance, holding period return is the total return on an asset or portfolio over the period during which it was held. It is one of the simplest measures of investment performance.
	Holding period return is the percentage by which the value of a portfolio has grown for a particular period.
Systematic risk	In finance and economics, systematic risk is vulnerability to events which affect aggregate outcomes such as broad market returns, total economy-wide resource holdings, or aggregate income. In many contexts, events like earthquakes and major weather catastrophes pose aggregate risks-they affect not only the distribution but also the total amount of resources. If every possible outcome of a stochastic economic process is characterized by the same aggregate result (but potentially different distributional outcomes), then the process has no aggregate risk.
Market risk	Market risk is the risk of losses in positions arising from movements in market prices. Some market risks include:•Equity risk, the risk that stock or stock indexes (e.g. Euro Stoxx 50, etc.) prices and/or their implied volatility will change•Interest rate risk, the risk that interest rates (e.g. Libor, Euribor, etc).
Deflation	In economics, deflation is a decrease in the general price level of goods and services. Deflation occurs when the inflation rate falls below 0% (a negative inflation rate). This should not be confused with disinflation, a slow-down in the inflation rate (i.e. when inflation declines to lower levels).
Revaluation	

Visit Cram101.com for full Practice Exams

5. Risk and Portfolio Management

CHAPTER HIGHLIGHTS & NOTES: KEY TERMS, PEOPLE, PLACES, CONCEPTS

	Revaluation means a rise of a price of goods or products. This term is specially used as revaluation of a currency, where it means a rise of currency to the relation with a foreign currency in a fixed exchange rate. In floating exchange rate correct term would be appreciation.
Business risks	Every business organization contains various risk elements while doing the business. Business risks implies uncertainty in profits or danger of loss and the events that could pose a risk due to some unforeseen events in future, which causes business to fail.

For example, an owner of a business may face different risks like in production,risks due to irregular supply of raw materials, machinery breakdown, labor unrest, etc.In marketing, risks may arise due to different market price fluctuations, changing trends and fashions,error in sales forecasting, etc.In addition, there may be loss of assets of the firm due to fire, flood, earthquakes, riots or war and political unrest which may cause unwanted interruptions in the business operations. |
| Collateral | In lending agreements, collateral is a borrower's pledge of specific property to a lender, to secure repayment of a loan. The collateral serves as protection for a lender against a borrower's default - that is, any borrower failing to pay the principal and interest under the terms of a loan obligation. If a borrower does default on a loan (due to insolvency or other event), that borrower forfeits (gives up) the property pledged as collateral - and the lender then becomes the owner of the collateral. |
| High-yield bond | In finance, a high-yield bond is a bond that is rated below investment grade. These bonds have a higher risk of default or other adverse credit events, but typically pay higher yields than better quality bonds in order to make them attractive to investors.

Global issue of high-yield bonds more than doubled in 2003 to nearly $146 billion in securities issued from less than $63 billion in 2002, although this is still less than the record of $150 billion in 1998. Issue is disproportionately centered in the United States, although issuers in Europe, Asia and South Africa have recently turned to high-yield debt in connection with refinancings and acquisitions. |
| Leverage | In negotiation, leverage is the ability to influence the other side to move closer to one's negotiating position.

Types of leverage include positive leverage, negative leverage, and normative leverage. Normative Leverage

Normative leverage is the application of general norms or the other party's standards and norms to advance one's own arguments for one's own good. |
| Diversification | Diversification is a form of corporate strategy for a company. |

Visit Cram101.com for full Practice Exams

5. Risk and Portfolio Management

CHAPTER HIGHLIGHTS & NOTES: KEY TERMS, PEOPLE, PLACES, CONCEPTS

	It seeks to increase profitability through greater sales volume obtained from new products and new markets. Diversification can occur either at the business unit level or at the corporate level.
Financial risk	Financial risk is an umbrella term for multiple types of risk associated with financing, including financial transactions that include company loans in risk of default. Risk is a term often used to imply downside risk, meaning the uncertainty of a return and the potential for financial loss. A science has evolved around managing market and financial risk under the general title of modern portfolio theory initiated by Dr. Harry Markowitz in 1952 with his article, 'Portfolio Selection'.
Standard deviation	In statistics and probability theory, standard deviation shows how much variation or 'dispersion' exists from the average (mean, or expected value). A low standard deviation indicates that the data points tend to be very close to the mean. High standard deviation indicates that the data points are spread out over a large range of values. The standard deviation of a random variable, statistical population, data set, or probability distribution is the square root of its variance. It is algebraically simpler though practically less robust than the average absolute deviation.
Semivariance	In spatial statistics, the empirical semivariance is described by $$\hat{\gamma}(h) = \frac{1}{2} \cdot \frac{1}{n(h)} \sum_{i=1}^{n(h)} (z(x_i + h) - z(x_i))^2$$ where z is a datum at a particular location, h is the distance between ordered data, and n(h) is the number of paired data at a distance of h. The semivariance is half the variance of the increments $z(x_i + h) - z(x_i)$, but the whole variance of z-values at given separation distance h (Bachmaier and Backes, 2008). A plot of semivariances versus distances between ordered data in a graph is known as a semivariogram rather than a variogram.
Coefficient of variation	In probability theory and statistics, the coefficient of variation is a normalized measure of dispersion of a probability distribution. It is also known as unitized risk or the variation coefficient. The absolute value of the CV is sometimes known as relative standard deviation (RSD), which is expressed as a percentage. The coefficient of variation (CV) is defined as the ratio of the standard deviation σ to the mean μ: $$c_v = \frac{\sigma}{\mu}$$

5. Risk and Portfolio Management

CHAPTER HIGHLIGHTS & NOTES: KEY TERMS, PEOPLE, PLACES, CONCEPTS

	which is the inverse of the signal-to-noise ratio. It shows the extent of variability in relation to mean of the population.
P3M3	P3M3, Programme and Project Management Maturity Model is a reference guide for structured best practice. It breaks down the broad disciplines of portfolio, programme and project management into a hierarchy of Key Process Areas (KPAs). The hierarchical approach enables organisations to assess their current capability and then plot a roadmap for improvement prioritised by those KPAs which will make the biggest impact on performance.
Covariance	In probability theory and statistics, covariance is a measure of how much two variables change together. Variance is a special case of the covariance when the two variables are identical.
Arbitrage pricing theory	In finance, arbitrage pricing theory is a general theory of asset pricing that holds that the expected return of a financial asset can be modeled as a linear function of various macro-economic factors or theoretical market indices, where sensitivity to changes in each factor is represented by a factor-specific beta coefficient. The model-derived rate of return will then be used to price the asset correctly - the asset price should equal the expected end of period price discounted at the rate implied by the model. If the price diverges, arbitrage should bring it back into line.
Asset allocation	Asset allocation is an investment strategy that attempts to balance risk versus reward by adjusting the percentage of each asset in an investment portfolio according to the investors risk tolerance, goals and investment time frame. Description
	Many financial experts say that asset allocation is an important factor in determining returns for an investment portfolio. Asset allocation is based on the principle that different assets perform differently in different market and economic conditions.
Capital asset pricing model	In finance, the capital asset pricing model is used to determine a theoretically appropriate required rate of return of an asset, if that asset is to be added to an already well-diversified portfolio, given that asset's non-diversifiable risk. The model takes into account the asset's sensitivity to non-diversifiable risk (also known as systematic risk or market risk), often represented by the quantity beta (β) in the financial industry, as well as the expected return of the market and the expected return of a theoretical risk-free asset.
	The model was introduced by Jack Treynor (1961, 1962), William Sharpe (1964), John Lintner (1965a,b) and Jan Mossin (1966) independently, building on the earlier work of Harry Markowitz on diversification and modern portfolio theory.
Efficient frontier	The efficient frontier is a concept in modern portfolio theory introduced by Harry Markowitz and others. A combination of assets, i.e.

5. Risk and Portfolio Management

CHAPTER HIGHLIGHTS & NOTES: KEY TERMS, PEOPLE, PLACES, CONCEPTS

a portfolio, is referred to as 'efficient' if it has the best possible expected level of return for its level of risk (usually proxied by the standard deviation of the portfolio's return). Here, every possible combination of risky assets, without including any holdings of the risk-free asset, can be plotted in risk-expected return space, and the collection of all such possible portfolios defines a region in this space.

Indifference curve	In microeconomic theory, an indifference curve is a graph showing different bundles of goods between which a consumer is indifferent. That is, at each point on the curve, the consumer has no preference for one bundle over another. One can equivalently refer to each point on the indifference curve as rendering the same level of utility (satisfaction) for the consumer.
Capital market line	Capital market line is the tangent line drawn from the point of the risk-free asset to the feasible region for risky assets. The tangency point M represents the market portfolio, so named since all rational investors (minimum variance criterion) should hold their risky assets in the same proportions as their weights in the market portfolio.

Formula
$$\mathrm{CML}: E(r) = r_f + \sigma \frac{E(r_M) - r_f}{\sigma_M}.$$

The Capital market line results from the combination of the market portfolio and the risk-free asset (the point L).

Security market line	Security market line is the representation of the Capital asset pricing model. It displays the expected rate of return of an individual security as a function of systematic, non-diversifiable risk (its beta). Formula

The Y-intercept of the security market line is equal to the risk-free interest rate. The slope of the Security market line is equal to the market risk premium and reflects the risk return trade off at a given time:
$$\mathrm{SML}: E(R_i) = R_f + \beta_i [E(R_M) - R_f]$$

Coefficient of determination	In statistics, the coefficient of determination is used in the context of statistical models whose main purpose is the prediction of future outcomes on the basis of other related information. It is the proportion of variability in a data set that is accounted for by the statistical model. It provides a measure of how well future outcomes are likely to be predicted by the model.
Value Line	Value Line is an independent investment research and financial publishing firm based in New York City, New York, USA, founded in 1931 by Arnold Bernhard. Value Line is best known for publishing The Value Line Investment Survey, a stock analysis newsletter that is updated weekly and kept by subscribers to the print edition in a large black or green binder. The company provides information via an online web page with both free and paid content.
Volatility	In finance, volatility is a measure for variation of price of a financial instrument over time.

5. Risk and Portfolio Management

CHAPTER HIGHLIGHTS & NOTES: KEY TERMS, PEOPLE, PLACES, CONCEPTS

	Historic volatility is derived from time series of past market prices. An implied volatility is derived from the market price of a market traded derivative (in particular an option).
Estimation	In project management (i.e., for engineering), accurate estimates are the basis of sound project planning. Many processes have been developed to aid engineers in making accurate estimates, such as•Analogy based estimation•Compartmentalization (i.e., breakdown of tasks)•Delphi method•Documenting estimation results•Educated assumptions•Estimating each task•Examining historical data•Identifying dependencies•Parametric estimating•Risk assessment•Structured planning
	Popular estimation processes for software projects include:•Cocomo•Cosysmo•Event chain methodology•Function points•Program Evaluation and Review Technique (PERT)•Proxy Based Estimation (PROBE) (from the Personal Software Process)•The Planning Game (from Extreme Programming)•Weighted Micro Function Points (WMFP)•Wideband Delphi.
Stock index	A stock index is a method of measuring the value of a section of the stock market. It is computed from the prices of selected stocks (sometimes a weighted average). It is a tool used by investors and financial managers to describe the market, and to compare the return on specific investments.
American Association of Individual Investors	The American Association of Individual Investors is a nonprofit organization with about 150,000 members whose purpose is to educate individual investors regarding stock market portolios, financial planning, and retirement accounts. AAII 'assists individuals in becoming effective managers of their own assets through programs of education, information and research.' The organization markets itself as an unbiased source of investment information because of its not-for-profit status.
	The organization was founded by James Cloonan, Ph.D. in 1978. Over the last thirty years, AAII's members report 'investment returns that are consistently higher than those of the stock market as a whole' (using the S&P 500 as reference).
Kurtosis	In probability theory and statistics, kurtosis is any measure of the 'peakedness' of the probability distribution of a real-valued random variable. In a similar way to the concept of skewness, kurtosis is a descriptor of the shape of a probability distribution and, just as for skewness, there are different ways of quantifying it for a theoretical distribution and corresponding ways of estimating it from a sample from a population.
	One common measure of kurtosis, originating with Karl Pearson, is based on a scaled version of the fourth moment of the data or population, but it has been argued that this measure really measures heavy tails, and not peakedness.

5. Risk and Portfolio Management

CHAPTER QUIZ: KEY TERMS, PEOPLE, PLACES, CONCEPTS

1. _____ is an independent investment research and financial publishing firm based in New York City, New York, USA, founded in 1931 by Arnold Bernhard. _____ is best known for publishing The _____ Investment Survey, a stock analysis newsletter that is updated weekly and kept by subscribers to the print edition in a large black or green binder. The company provides information via an online web page with both free and paid content.

   a. Value transfer system
   b. Wall Street Journal prime rate
   c. Value Line
   d. Reserve ratio

2. A _____ is a profit that results from a disposition of a capital asset, such as stock, bond or real estate, where the amount realized on the disposition exceeds the purchase price. The gain is the difference between a higher selling price and a lower purchase price. Conversely, a capital loss arises if the proceeds from the sale of a capital asset are less than the purchase price.

   a. Capital gains tax
   b. granularity
   c. Capital gain
   d. Stiglitz

3. The _____ is the expected value of a random variable usually representing a gain, i.e. the weighted-average outcome in gambling, probability theory, economics or finance.

   It is calculated by using the following formula:

   How do you calculate the average of a probability distribution? As denoted by the above formula, simply take the probability of each possible return outcome and multiply it by the return outcome itself. For example, if you knew a given investment had a 50% chance of earning a 10 return, a 25% chance of earning 20 and a 25% chance of earning -10, the _____ would be equal to 7.5:

   Although this is what you expect the return to be, there is no guarantee that it will be the actual return.

   a. Experiment
   b. Impossibility of a gambling system
   c. Expected return
   d. Inclusion-exclusion principle

4. . In finance, a _____ is a bond that is rated below investment grade. These bonds have a higher risk of default or other adverse credit events, but typically pay higher yields than better quality bonds in order to make them attractive to investors.

   Global issue of _____s more than doubled in 2003 to nearly $146 billion in securities issued from less than $63 billion in 2002, although this is still less than the record of $150 billion in 1998.

Visit Cram101.com for full Practice Exams

5. Risk and Portfolio Management

CHAPTER QUIZ: KEY TERMS, PEOPLE, PLACES, CONCEPTS

Issue is disproportionately centered in the United States, although issuers in Europe, Asia and South Africa have recently turned to high-yield debt in connection with refinancings and acquisitions.

a. Business Development Company
b. Club deal
c. Firstpex
d. High-yield bond

5. Saving accounts are accounts maintained by retail financial institutions that pay interest but cannot be used directly as money in the narrow sense of a medium of exchange (for example, by writing a cheque). These accounts let customers set aside a portion of their liquid assets while earning a monetary return. For the bank, money in a _____ may not be callable immediately and in some jurisdictions, does not incur a reserve requirement, freeing up cash from the bank's vault to be lent out with interest.

a. Service release premium
b. Savings account
c. Single Supervisory Mechanism
d. Soft probe

ANSWER KEY
5. Risk and Portfolio Management

1. c
2. c
3. c
4. d
5. b

You can take the complete Chapter Practice Test

for 5. Risk and Portfolio Management
on all key terms, persons, places, and concepts.

Online 99 Cents

http://www.epub2174.13.22362.5.cram101.com/

Use www.Cram101.com for all your study needs

including Cram101's online interactive problem solving labs in

chemistry, statistics, mathematics, and more.

Visit Cram101.com for full Practice Exams

6. Investment Companies: Mutual Funds

CHAPTER OUTLINE: KEY TERMS, PEOPLE, PLACES, CONCEPTS

- Dividend reinvestment plan
- Leverage
- Net asset value
- Growth investing
- Investment style
- P3M3
- Contrarian
- Style investing
- Value Line
- Stock valuation
- American Association of Individual Investors
- Socially responsible investing
- High-yield bond
- Exchange-traded fund
- Money market fund
- Commercial paper
- Federal Deposit Insurance Corporation
- Stock index
- Investment Advisers Act of 1940
- Capital gain
- Benchmarking

Visit Cram101.com for full Practice Exams

6. Investment Companies: Mutual Funds
CHAPTER OUTLINE: KEY TERMS, PEOPLE, PLACES, CONCEPTS

	Capital asset pricing model
	Security market line
	Systematic risk
	Limited liability

CHAPTER HIGHLIGHTS & NOTES: KEY TERMS, PEOPLE, PLACES, CONCEPTS

Dividend reinvestment plan	A dividend reinvestment program or dividend reinvestment plan is an equity investment option offered directly from the underlying company. The investor does not receive quarterly dividends directly as cash; instead, the investor's dividends are directly reinvested in the underlying equity. (The investor must still pay tax annually on his or her dividend income, whether it is received or reinvested).
Leverage	In negotiation, leverage is the ability to influence the other side to move closer to one's negotiating position. Types of leverage include positive leverage, negative leverage, and normative leverage. Normative Leverage Normative leverage is the application of general norms or the other party's standards and norms to advance one's own arguments for one's own good.
Net asset value	Net asset value is the value of an entity's assets less the value of its liabilities, often in relation to open-end or mutual funds, since shares of such funds registered with the U.S. Securities and Exchange Commission are redeemed at their net asset value. This may also be the same as the book value or the equity value of a business. Net asset value may represent the value of the total equity, or it may be divided by the number of shares outstanding held by investors and, thereby, represent the net asset value per share.
Growth investing	Growth investing is a style of investment strategy. Those who follow this style, known as growth investors, invest in companies that exhibit signs of above-average growth, even if the share price appears expensive in terms of metrics such as price-to-earnings or price-to-book ratios. In typical usage, the term 'growth investing' contrasts with the strategy known as value investing.

Visit Cram101.com for full Practice Exams

6. Investment Companies: Mutual Funds

CHAPTER HIGHLIGHTS & NOTES: KEY TERMS, PEOPLE, PLACES, CONCEPTS

Investment style	Investment style refers to different style characteristics of equities, bonds or financial derivatives within a given investment philosophy. Theory would favor a combination of big capitalization, passive and value. Of course one could almost get that when investing in an important Index like S&P 500, EURO STOXX or the like.
P3M3	P3M3, Programme and Project Management Maturity Model is a reference guide for structured best practice. It breaks down the broad disciplines of portfolio, programme and project management into a hierarchy of Key Process Areas (KPAs). The hierarchical approach enables organisations to assess their current capability and then plot a roadmap for improvement prioritised by those KPAs which will make the biggest impact on performance.
Contrarian	In finance, a contrarian is one who attempts to profit by investing in a manner that differs from the conventional wisdom, when the consensus opinion appears to be wrong. A contrarian believes that certain crowd behavior among investors can lead to exploitable mispricings in securities markets. For example, widespread pessimism about a stock can drive a price so low that it overstates the company's risks, and understates its prospects for returning to profitability.
Style investing	Style investing is an investment approach in which rotation among different 'styles' is supposed to be important for successful investing. As opposed to investing in individual securities, style investors can decide to make portfolio allocation decisions by placing their money in broad categories of assets, such as 'large-cap', 'growth', 'international', or 'emerging markets'. Style investing is of interest to economists because it serves as a useful framework for identifying anomalous price movements in stocks, such as those observed when a stock is added or removed from the S&P 500 index.
Value Line	Value Line is an independent investment research and financial publishing firm based in New York City, New York, USA, founded in 1931 by Arnold Bernhard. Value Line is best known for publishing The Value Line Investment Survey, a stock analysis newsletter that is updated weekly and kept by subscribers to the print edition in a large black or green binder. The company provides information via an online web page with both free and paid content.
Stock valuation	In financial markets, stock valuation is the method of calculating theoretical values of companies and their stocks. The main use of these methods is to predict future market prices, or more generally, potential market prices, and thus to profit from price movement - stocks that are judged undervalued (with respect to their theoretical value) are bought, while stocks that are judged overvalued are sold, in the expectation that undervalued stocks will, on the whole, rise in value, while overvalued stocks will, on the whole, fall.

Visit Cram101.com for full Practice Exams

6. Investment Companies: Mutual Funds

CHAPTER HIGHLIGHTS & NOTES: KEY TERMS, PEOPLE, PLACES, CONCEPTS

American Association of Individual Investors	The American Association of Individual Investors is a nonprofit organization with about 150,000 members whose purpose is to educate individual investors regarding stock market portolios, financial planning, and retirement accounts. AAII 'assists individuals in becoming effective managers of their own assets through programs of education, information and research.' The organization markets itself as an unbiased source of investment information because of its not-for-profit status. The organization was founded by James Cloonan, Ph.D. in 1978. Over the last thirty years, AAII's members report 'investment returns that are consistently higher than those of the stock market as a whole' (using the S&P 500 as reference).
Socially responsible investing	Socially responsible investing also known as sustainable, socially conscious, green or ethical investing, is any investment strategy which seeks to consider both financial return and social good. In general, socially responsible investors encourage corporate practices that promote environmental stewardship, consumer protection, human rights, and diversity. Some avoid businesses involved in alcohol, tobacco, gambling, pornography, weapons, and/or the military.
High-yield bond	In finance, a high-yield bond is a bond that is rated below investment grade. These bonds have a higher risk of default or other adverse credit events, but typically pay higher yields than better quality bonds in order to make them attractive to investors. Global issue of high-yield bonds more than doubled in 2003 to nearly $146 billion in securities issued from less than $63 billion in 2002, although this is still less than the record of $150 billion in 1998. Issue is disproportionately centered in the United States, although issuers in Europe, Asia and South Africa have recently turned to high-yield debt in connection with refinancings and acquisitions.
Exchange-traded fund	An exchange-traded fund is an investment fund traded on stock exchanges, much like stocks. An ETF holds assets such as stocks, commodities, or bonds, and trades close to its net asset value over the course of the trading day. Most ETFs track an index, such as the S&P 500 or MSCI EAFE. ETFs may be attractive as investments because of their low costs, tax efficiency, and stock-like features.
Money market fund	A money market fund is an open-ended mutual fund that invests in short-term debt securities such as US Treasury bills and commercial paper. Money market funds are widely (though not necessarily accurately) regarded as being as safe as bank deposits yet providing a higher yield. Regulated in the US under the Investment Company Act of 1940, money market funds are important providers of liquidity to financial intermediaries.
Commercial paper	In the global money market, commercial paper is an unsecured promissory note with a fixed maturity of 1 to 365 days.

Visit Cram101.com for full Practice Exams

6. Investment Companies: Mutual Funds

CHAPTER HIGHLIGHTS & NOTES: KEY TERMS, PEOPLE, PLACES, CONCEPTS

	Commercial paper is a money-market security issued (sold) by large corporations to get money to meet short term debt obligations (for example, payroll), and is only backed by an issuing bank or corporation's promise to pay the face amount on the maturity date specified on the note. Since it is not backed by collateral, only firms with excellent credit ratings from a recognized rating agency will be able to sell their commercial paper at a reasonable price.
Federal Deposit Insurance Corporation	The Federal Deposit Insurance Corporation is a United States government corporation created by the Glass-Steagall Act of 1933. It provides deposit insurance, which guarantees the safety of deposits in member banks, up to $250,000 per depositor per bank as of January 2012. As of November 18, 2010 (2010 -11-18), the federal\ deposit\ insurance\ corporation insured deposits at 7,723 institutions. The federal\ deposit\ insurance\ corporation also examines and supervises certain financial institutions for safety and soundness, performs certain consumer-protection functions, and manages banks in receiverships (failed banks). Insured institutions are required to place signs at their place of business stating that 'deposits are backed by the full faith and credit of the United States Government.' Since the start of federal\ deposit\ insurance\ corporation insurance on January 1, 1934, no depositor has lost any insured funds as a result of a failure.
Stock index	A stock index is a method of measuring the value of a section of the stock market. It is computed from the prices of selected stocks (sometimes a weighted average). It is a tool used by investors and financial managers to describe the market, and to compare the return on specific investments.
Investment Advisers Act of 1940	The Investment Advisers Act of 1940, codified at 15 U.S.C. § 80b-1 through 15 U.S.C. § 80b-21, is a United States federal law that was created to regulate the actions of investment advisers (also spelled 'advisors') as defined by the law. Overview The law provides in part: Contents The Investment Advisers Act (IAA) was passed in 1940 in order to monitor those who, for a fee, advise people, pension funds, and institutions on investment matters. Impetus for passage of the act began with the Public Utility Holding Company Act of 1935 which authorized the Securities and Exchange Commission (SEC) to study investment trusts.
Capital gain	A capital gain is a profit that results from a disposition of a capital asset, such as stock, bond or real estate, where the amount realized on the disposition exceeds the purchase price. The gain is the difference between a higher selling price and a lower purchase price. Conversely, a capital loss arises if the proceeds from the sale of a capital asset are less than the purchase price.
Benchmarking	Benchmarking is the process of comparing one's business processes and performance metrics to industry bests or best practices from other industries. Dimensions typically measured are quality, time and cost.

Visit Cram101.com for full Practice Exams

6. Investment Companies: Mutual Funds

CHAPTER HIGHLIGHTS & NOTES: KEY TERMS, PEOPLE, PLACES, CONCEPTS

Capital asset pricing model	In finance, the capital asset pricing model is used to determine a theoretically appropriate required rate of return of an asset, if that asset is to be added to an already well-diversified portfolio, given that asset's non-diversifiable risk. The model takes into account the asset's sensitivity to non-diversifiable risk (also known as systematic risk or market risk), often represented by the quantity beta (β) in the financial industry, as well as the expected return of the market and the expected return of a theoretical risk-free asset. The model was introduced by Jack Treynor (1961, 1962), William Sharpe (1964), John Lintner (1965a,b) and Jan Mossin (1966) independently, building on the earlier work of Harry Markowitz on diversification and modern portfolio theory.
Security market line	Security market line is the representation of the Capital asset pricing model. It displays the expected rate of return of an individual security as a function of systematic, non-diversifiable risk (its beta). Formula The Y-intercept of the security market line is equal to the risk-free interest rate. The slope of the Security market line is equal to the market risk premium and reflects the risk return trade off at a given time: $\mathrm{SML}: E(R_i) = R_f + \beta_i[E(R_M) - R_f]$
Systematic risk	In finance and economics, systematic risk is vulnerability to events which affect aggregate outcomes such as broad market returns, total economy-wide resource holdings, or aggregate income. In many contexts, events like earthquakes and major weather catastrophes pose aggregate risks-they affect not only the distribution but also the total amount of resources. If every possible outcome of a stochastic economic process is characterized by the same aggregate result (but potentially different distributional outcomes), then the process has no aggregate risk.
Limited liability	Limited liability is a concept whereby a person's financial liability is limited to a fixed sum, most commonly the value of a person's investment in a company or partnership with limited liability. If a company with limited liability is sued, then the plaintiffs are suing the company, not its owners or investors. A shareholder in a limited company is not personally liable for any of the debts of the company, other than for the value of their investment in that company.

Visit Cram101.com for full Practice Exams

6. Investment Companies: Mutual Funds

CHAPTER QUIZ: KEY TERMS, PEOPLE, PLACES, CONCEPTS

1. _____ is the representation of the Capital asset pricing model. It displays the expected rate of return of an individual security as a function of systematic, non-diversifiable risk (its beta). Formula

   The Y-intercept of the _____ is equal to the risk-free interest rate. The slope of the _____ is equal to the market risk premium and reflects the risk return trade off at a given time: $SML : E(R_i) = R_f + \beta_i[E(R_M) - R_f]$

   a. Security market line
   b. Benefits realisation management
   c. Binary option
   d. Bond credit rating

2. _____ is the process of comparing one's business processes and performance metrics to industry bests or best practices from other industries. Dimensions typically measured are quality, time and cost. In the process of best practice _____, management identifies the best firms in their industry, or in another industry where similar processes exist, and compares the results and processes of those studied (the 'targets') to one's own results and processes.

   a. Benchmarking e-learning
   b. BSC SWOT
   c. Business System Planning
   d. Benchmarking

3. In finance, a _____ is a bond that is rated below investment grade. These bonds have a higher risk of default or other adverse credit events, but typically pay higher yields than better quality bonds in order to make them attractive to investors.

   Global issue of _____s more than doubled in 2003 to nearly $146 billion in securities issued from less than $63 billion in 2002, although this is still less than the record of $150 billion in 1998. Issue is disproportionately centered in the United States, although issuers in Europe, Asia and South Africa have recently turned to high-yield debt in connection with refinancings and acquisitions.

   a. Business Development Company
   b. High-yield bond
   c. Firstpex
   d. Growth capital

4. . _____ is a concept whereby a person's financial liability is limited to a fixed sum, most commonly the value of a person's investment in a company or partnership with _____. If a company with _____ is sued, then the plaintiffs are suing the company, not its owners or investors. A shareholder in a limited company is not personally liable for any of the debts of the company, other than for the value of their investment in that company.

   a. Market area
   b. Limited liability
   c. Model audit

Visit Cram101.com for full Practice Exams

6. Investment Companies: Mutual Funds

CHAPTER QUIZ: KEY TERMS, PEOPLE, PLACES, CONCEPTS

5. An _____ is an investment fund traded on stock exchanges, much like stocks. An ETF holds assets such as stocks, commodities, or bonds, and trades close to its net asset value over the course of the trading day. Most ETFs track an index, such as the S&P 500 or MSCI EAFE. ETFs may be attractive as investments because of their low costs, tax efficiency, and stock-like features.

- a. Icapital.biz Berhad
- b. IFund
- c. Income fund
- d. Exchange-traded fund

ANSWER KEY
6. Investment Companies: Mutual Funds

1. a
2. d
3. b
4. b
5. d

You can take the complete Chapter Practice Test

for 6. Investment Companies: Mutual Funds
on all key terms, persons, places, and concepts.

Online 99 Cents

http://www.epub2174.13.22362.6.cram101.com/

Use www.Cram101.com for all your study needs

including Cram101's online interactive problem solving labs in

chemistry, statistics, mathematics, and more.

7. Closed-end Investment Companies, Real Estate Investment Trusts

CHAPTER OUTLINE: KEY TERMS, PEOPLE, PLACES, CONCEPTS

- Net asset value
- Unit trust
- Real estate investment trust
- Debt ratio
- Securitization
- Exchange-traded fund
- Stock index
- Perpetual bond
- Tracking error
- Financial Industry Regulatory Authority
- Short sale
- Hedge fund
- Private equity fund
- Sarbanes-Oxley Act

7. Closed-end Investment Companies, Real Estate Investment Trusts

CHAPTER HIGHLIGHTS & NOTES: KEY TERMS, PEOPLE, PLACES, CONCEPTS

Net asset value	Net asset value is the value of an entity's assets less the value of its liabilities, often in relation to open-end or mutual funds, since shares of such funds registered with the U.S. Securities and Exchange Commission are redeemed at their net asset value. This may also be the same as the book value or the equity value of a business. Net asset value may represent the value of the total equity, or it may be divided by the number of shares outstanding held by investors and, thereby, represent the net asset value per share.
Unit trust	A unit trust is a form of collective investment constituted under a trust deed. Found in Australia, Ireland, the Isle of Man, Jersey, New Zealand, Namibia, South Africa, Singapore, Malaysia and the UK, unit trusts offer access to a wide range of securities. Unit trusts are open-ended investments; therefore the underlying value of the assets is always directly represented by the total number of units issued multiplied by the unit price less the transaction or management fee charged and any other associated costs.
Real estate investment trust	A real estate investment trust is a tax designation for a corporate entity investing in real estate. The purpose of this designation is to reduce or eliminate corporate tax. In return, Real estate investment trusts are required to distribute at least 90% of their taxable income into the hands of investors.
Debt ratio	Debt Ratio is a financial ratio that indicates the percentage of a company's assets that are provided via debt. It is the ratio of total debt (the sum of current liabilities and long-term liabilities) and total assets (the sum of current assets, fixed assets, and other assets such as 'goodwill'). $$\text{Debt ratio} = \frac{\text{Total Debt}}{\text{Total Assets}}$$ or alternatively: $$\text{Debt ratio} = \frac{\text{Total Liability}}{\text{Total Assets}}$$ For example, a company with $2 million in total assets and $500,000 in total liabilities would have a debt ratio of 25%.
Securitization	Securitization is the financial practice of pooling various types of contractual debt such as residential mortgages, commercial mortgages, auto loans or credit card debt obligations and selling said consolidated debt as bonds, pass-through securities, or Collateralized mortgage obligation (CMOs), to various investors. The principal and interest on the debt, underlying the security, is paid back to the various investors regularly.

7. Closed-end Investment Companies, Real Estate Investment Trusts

CHAPTER HIGHLIGHTS & NOTES: KEY TERMS, PEOPLE, PLACES, CONCEPTS

Exchange-traded fund	An exchange-traded fund is an investment fund traded on stock exchanges, much like stocks. An ETF holds assets such as stocks, commodities, or bonds, and trades close to its net asset value over the course of the trading day. Most ETFs track an index, such as the S&P 500 or MSCI EAFE. ETFs may be attractive as investments because of their low costs, tax efficiency, and stock-like features.
Stock index	A stock index is a method of measuring the value of a section of the stock market. It is computed from the prices of selected stocks (sometimes a weighted average). It is a tool used by investors and financial managers to describe the market, and to compare the return on specific investments.
Perpetual bond	Perpetual bond, which is also known as a Perpetual or just a Perp, is a bond with no maturity date. Therefore, it may be treated as equity, not as debt. Perpetual bonds pay coupons forever, and the issuer does not have to redeem them.
Tracking error	In finance, tracking error is a measure of how closely a portfolio follows the index to which it is benchmarked. The best measure is the root-mean-square of the difference between the portfolio and index returns. Many portfolios are managed to a benchmark, typically an index.
Financial Industry Regulatory Authority	In the United States, the Financial Industry Regulatory Authority, Inc., or FINRA, is a private corporation that acts as a self-regulatory organization (SRO). FINRA is the successor to the National Association of Securities Dealers, Inc. (NASD).
Short sale	A short sale is a sale of real estate in which the sale proceeds fall short of the balance owed on the property's loan. It often occurs when a borrower cannot pay the mortgage loan on their property, but the lender decides that selling the property at a moderate loss is better than pressing the borrower. Both parties consent to the short sale process, because it allows them to avoid foreclosure, which involves hefty fees for the bank and poorer credit report outcomes for the borrowers.
Hedge fund	Hedge funds are private, actively managed investment funds. They invest in a diverse range of markets, investment instruments, and strategies and are subject to the regulatory restrictions of their country. U.S. regulations limit hedge fund participation to certain classes of accredited investors.
Private equity fund	A private equity fund is a collective investment scheme used for making investments in various equity (and to a lesser extent debt) securities according to one of the investment strategies associated with private equity. Private equity funds are typically limited partnerships with a fixed term of 10 years (often with annual extensions). At inception, institutional investors make an unfunded commitment to the limited partnership, which is then drawn over the term of the fund.
Sarbanes-Oxley Act	The Sarbanes-Oxley Act of 2002 (Pub.L.

Visit Cram101.com for full Practice Exams

7. Closed-end Investment Companies, Real Estate Investment Trusts

CHAPTER HIGHLIGHTS & NOTES: KEY TERMS, PEOPLE, PLACES, CONCEPTS

107-204, 116 Stat. 745, enacted July 29, 2002), also known as the 'Public Company Accounting Reform and Investor Protection Act' (in the Senate) and 'Corporate and Auditing Accountability and Responsibility Act' (in the House) and more commonly called Sarbanes-Oxley, Sarbox or SOX, is a United States federal law that set new or enhanced standards for all U.S. public company boards, management and public accounting firms. ponsors U.S. Senator Paul Sarbanes (D-MD) and U.S. Representative Michael G. Oxley (R-OH). As a result of SOX, top management must now individually certify the accuracy of financial information.

CHAPTER QUIZ: KEY TERMS, PEOPLE, PLACES, CONCEPTS

1. _____ is a financial ratio that indicates the percentage of a company's assets that are provided via debt. It is the ratio of total debt (the sum of current liabilities and long-term liabilities) and total assets (the sum of current assets, fixed assets, and other assets such as 'goodwill').

$$\text{Debt ratio} = \frac{\text{Total Debt}}{\text{Total Assets}}$$

or alternatively:

$$\text{Debt ratio} = \frac{\text{Total Liability}}{\text{Total Assets}}$$

For example, a company with $2 million in total assets and $500,000 in total liabilities would have a _____ of 25%.

a. Debt service ratio
b. Debt ratio
c. Debt-to-equity ratio
d. Debt-to-GDP ratio

2. . _____ is the value of an entity's assets less the value of its liabilities, often in relation to open-end or mutual funds, since shares of such funds registered with the U.S. Securities and Exchange Commission are redeemed at their _____. This may also be the same as the book value or the equity value of a business. _____ may represent the value of the total equity, or it may be divided by the number of shares outstanding held by investors and, thereby, represent the _____ per share.

a. Neuberger Berman
b. Passive management

Visit Cram101.com for full Practice Exams

7. Closed-end Investment Companies, Real Estate Investment Trusts

CHAPTER QUIZ: KEY TERMS, PEOPLE, PLACES, CONCEPTS

   c. Payment service provider
   d. Net asset value

3. A _____ is a form of collective investment constituted under a trust deed.

   Found in Australia, Ireland, the Isle of Man, Jersey, New Zealand, Namibia, South Africa, Singapore, Malaysia and the UK, _____ s offer access to a wide range of securities.

   _____ s are open-ended investments; therefore the underlying value of the assets is always directly represented by the total number of units issued multiplied by the unit price less the transaction or management fee charged and any other associated costs.

   a. Unitised insurance fund
   b. Open-end fund
   c. Unit trust
   d. Payment Services Directive

4. A _____ is a tax designation for a corporate entity investing in real estate. The purpose of this designation is to reduce or eliminate corporate tax. In return, _____ s are required to distribute at least 90% of their taxable income into the hands of investors.

   a. Real estate investment trust
   b. Open-end fund
   c. Jimmy Carter
   d. Payment Services Directive

5. _____ is the financial practice of pooling various types of contractual debt such as residential mortgages, commercial mortgages, auto loans or credit card debt obligations and selling said consolidated debt as bonds, pass-through securities, or Collateralized mortgage obligation (CMOs), to various investors. The principal and interest on the debt, underlying the security, is paid back to the various investors regularly. Securities backed by mortgage receivables are called mortgage-backed securities (MBS), while those backed by other types of receivables are asset-backed securities (ABS).

   a. Securitization
   b. Seeking Alpha
   c. Selling away
   d. Settlement

Visit Cram101.com for full Practice Exams

ANSWER KEY
7. Closed-end Investment Companies, Real Estate Investment Trusts

1. b
2. d
3. c
4. a
5. a

You can take the complete Chapter Practice Test

for 7. Closed-end Investment Companies, Real Estate Investment Trusts
on all key terms, persons, places, and concepts.

Online 99 Cents

http://www.epub2174.13.22362.7.cram101.com/

Use www.Cram101.com for all your study needs

including Cram101's online interactive problem solving labs in

chemistry, statistics, mathematics, and more.

8. Stock

CHAPTER OUTLINE: KEY TERMS, PEOPLE, PLACES, CONCEPTS

- Board of directors
- Certificate of incorporation
- Common stock
- Equity
- Preferred stock
- Cumulative voting
- Director
- Business risks
- Real estate investment trust
- Retention ratio
- Ex-dividend date
- Dividend reinvestment plan
- Dividend
- Balance sheet
- Stock split
- Reverse stock split
- Stock repurchase
- Liquidation
- Annual report
- Asset
- Long-term liabilities

Visit Cram101.com for full Practice Exams

8. Stock

CHAPTER OUTLINE: KEY TERMS, PEOPLE, PLACES, CONCEPTS

- Current ratio
- Income statement
- Operating income
- Hedge fund
- Accelerated depreciation
- Accounts receivable
- Quick ratio
- Inventory turnover
- Days sales outstanding
- Net profit margin
- Operating margin
- Return on assets
- Return on equity
- Debt-to-equity ratio
- Financial risk
- Debt ratio
- Cash flow statement

Visit Cram101.com for full Practice Exams

8. Stock

CHAPTER HIGHLIGHTS & NOTES: KEY TERMS, PEOPLE, PLACES, CONCEPTS

Board of directors	A board of directors is a body of elected or appointed members who jointly oversee the activities of a company or organization. Other names include board of governors, board of managers, board of regents, board of trustees, and board of visitors. It is often simply referred to as 'the board'.
Certificate of incorporation	A certificate of incorporation is a legal document relating to the formation of a company or corporation. It is a license to form a corporation issued by state government. Its precise meaning depends upon the legal system in which it is used, but the two primary meanings are: Commonwealth systems In the U.S.A. a certificate of incorporation is usually used as an alternative description of a corporation's articles of incorporation.
Common stock	Common stock is a form of corporate equity ownership, a type of security. The terms 'voting share' or 'ordinary share' are also used in other parts of the world; common stock being primarily used in the United States. It is called 'common' to distinguish it from preferred stock.
Equity	Equity or Economic equality, is the concept or idea of fairness in economics, particularly as to taxation or welfare economics. More specifically it may refer to equal life chances regardless of identity, to provide all citizens with a basic and equal minimum of income/goods/services or to increase funds and commitment for redistribution. Inequality and inequities have significantly increased in recent decades, possibly driven by the worldwide economic processes of globalisation, economic liberalisation and integration.
Preferred stock	Preferred stock is an equity security which may have any combination of features not possessed by common stock including properties of both an equity and a debt instruments, and is generally considered a hybrid instrument. Preferreds are senior (i.e. higher ranking) to common stock, but subordinate to bonds in terms of claim . Preferred stock usually carries no voting rights, but may carry a dividend and may have priority over common stock in the payment of dividends and upon liquidation.
Cumulative voting	Cumulative voting is a multiple-winner voting system intended to promote more proportional representation than winner-take-all elections. Cumulative voting is used frequently in corporate governance, where it is mandated by some (7) U.S. states. It was used to elect the Illinois House of Representatives from 1870 until its repeal in 1980 and used in England in the late 19th century to elect some school boards.
Director	Director refers to a rank in management.

Visit Cram101.com for full Practice Exams

8. Stock

CHAPTER HIGHLIGHTS & NOTES: KEY TERMS, PEOPLE, PLACES, CONCEPTS

	A director is a person who leads, or supervises a certain area of a company, a program, or a project. Usually companies, which use this title commonly have large numbers of people with the title of director with different categories (e.g. director of human resources).
Business risks	Every business organization contains various risk elements while doing the business. Business risks implies uncertainty in profits or danger of loss and the events that could pose a risk due to some unforeseen events in future, which causes business to fail.
	For example, an owner of a business may face different risks like in production,risks due to irregular supply of raw materials, machinery breakdown, labor unrest, etc.In marketing, risks may arise due to different market price fluctuations, changing trends and fashions,error in sales forecasting, etc.In addition, there may be loss of assets of the firm due to fire, flood, earthquakes, riots or war and political unrest which may cause unwanted interruptions in the business operations.
Real estate investment trust	A real estate investment trust is a tax designation for a corporate entity investing in real estate. The purpose of this designation is to reduce or eliminate corporate tax. In return, Real estate investment trusts are required to distribute at least 90% of their taxable income into the hands of investors.
Retention ratio	Retention Ratio indicates the percentage of a company's earnings that are not paid out in dividends but credited to retained earnings. It is the opposite of the dividend payout ratio, so that also called the retention rate.
	Retention Ratio = 1 - Dividend Payout Ratio = Retained Earnings / Net Income
	Retention ratio is also called plowback ratio.
Ex-dividend date	The ex-dividend date, is an investment term involving the timing of payment of dividends on stocks of corporations, income trusts, and other financial holdings, both publicly and privately held.
	In the United States, the IRS defines the ex-dividend date as 'the first date following the declaration of a dividend on which the buyer of a stock is not entitled to receive the next dividend payment.' The London Stock Exchange defines the term 'ex' as 'when a stock or dividend is issued by a company it is based upon an 'on register' or 'record date'. However, to create a level playing field when shares are traded on the London Stock Exchange during this benefit period an 'ex' date is set.
Dividend reinvestment plan	A dividend reinvestment program or dividend reinvestment plan is an equity investment option offered directly from the underlying company. The investor does not receive quarterly dividends directly as cash; instead, the investor's dividends are directly reinvested in the underlying equity.

Visit Cram101.com for full Practice Exams

8. Stock

CHAPTER HIGHLIGHTS & NOTES: KEY TERMS, PEOPLE, PLACES, CONCEPTS

Dividend	Dividends are payments made by a corporation to its shareholder members. It is the portion of corporate profits paid out to stockholders. When a corporation earns a profit or surplus, that money can be put to two uses: it can either be re-invested in the business (called retained earnings), or it can be distributed to shareholders.
Balance sheet	In financial accounting, a balance sheet is a summary of the financial balances of a sole proprietorship, a business partnership, a corporation or other business organization, such as an LLC or an LLP. Assets, liabilities and ownership equity are listed as of a specific date, such as the end of its financial year. A balance sheet is often described as a 'snapshot of a company's financial condition'. Of the four basic financial statements, the balance sheet is the only statement which applies to a single point in time of a business' calendar year.
Stock split	A stock split or stock divide increases the number of shares in a public company. The price is adjusted such that the before and after market capitalization of the company remains the same and dilution does not occur. Options and warrants are included.
Reverse stock split	On a stock exchange, a reverse stock split are subsequently canceled. A reverse stock split is also called a stock merge. The reduction in the number of issued shares is accompanied by a proportional increase in the share price.
Stock repurchase	Stock repurchase is the reacquisition by a company of its own stock. In some countries, including the U.S. and the UK, a corporation can repurchase its own stock by distributing cash to existing shareholders in exchange for a fraction of the company's outstanding equity; that is, cash is exchanged for a reduction in the number of shares outstanding. The company either retires the repurchased shares or keeps them as treasury stock, available for re-issuance.
Liquidation	In law, liquidation is the process by which a company is brought to an end, and the assets and property of the company redistributed. Liquidation is also sometimes referred to as winding-up or dissolution, although dissolution technically refers to the last stage of liquidation. The process of liquidation also arises when customs, an authority or agency in a country responsible for collecting and safeguarding customs duties, determines the final computation or ascertainment of the duties or drawback accruing on an entry.
Annual report	An annual report is a comprehensive report on a company's activities throughout the preceding year. Annual reports are intended to give shareholders and other interested people information about the company's activities and financial performance. Most jurisdictions require companies to prepare and disclose annual reports, and many require the annual report to be filed at the company's registry.
Asset	In financial accounting, assets are economic resources. Anything tangible or intangible that is capable of being owned or controlled to produce value and that is held to have positive economic value is considered an asset.

8. Stock

CHAPTER HIGHLIGHTS & NOTES: KEY TERMS, PEOPLE, PLACES, CONCEPTS

Long-term liabilities	Long-term liabilities are liabilities with a future benefit over one year, such as notes payable that mature longer than one year.
	In accounting, the long-term liabilities are shown on the right wing of the balance-sheet representing the sources of funds, which are generally bounded in form of capital assets.
	Examples of long-term liabilities are debentures, mortgage loans and other bank loans.
Current ratio	The current ratio is a financial ratio that measures whether or not a firm has enough resources to pay its debts over the next 12 months. It compares a firm's current assets to its current liabilities. It is expressed as follows:
	$$\text{Current ratio} = \frac{\text{Current Assets}}{\text{Current Liabilities}}$$
	The current ratio is an indication of a firm's market liquidity and ability to meet creditor's demands.
Income statement	An income statement or profit and loss account (also referred to as a profit and loss statement (P&L), revenue statement, statement of financial performance, earnings statement, operating statement, or statement of operations) is one of the financial statements of a company and shows the company's revenues and expenses during a particular period. It indicates how the revenues (money received from the sale of products and services before expenses are taken out, also known as the 'top line') are transformed into the net income (the result after all revenues and expenses have been accounted for, also known as 'net profit' or the 'bottom line'). It displays the revenues recognized for a specific period, and the cost and expenses charged against these revenues, including write-offs (e.g., depreciation and amortization of various assets) and taxes.
Operating income	In accounting and finance, earnings before interest and taxes (EBIT), also called operating profit or operating income is a measure of a firm's profit that excludes interest and income tax expenses. It is the difference between operating revenues and operating expenses. When a firm does not have non-operating income, then operating income is sometimes used as a synonym for EBIT and operating profit.
Hedge fund	Hedge funds are private, actively managed investment funds. They invest in a diverse range of markets, investment instruments, and strategies and are subject to the regulatory restrictions of their country. U.S. regulations limit hedge fund participation to certain classes of accredited investors.
Accelerated depreciation	Accelerated depreciation refers to any one of several methods by which a company, for 'financial accounting' or tax purposes, depreciates a fixed asset in such a way that the amount of depreciation taken each year is higher during the earlier years of an asset's life.

8. Stock

CHAPTER HIGHLIGHTS & NOTES: KEY TERMS, PEOPLE, PLACES, CONCEPTS

	For financial accounting purposes, accelerated depreciation is generally used when an asset is expected to be much more productive during its early years, so that depreciation expense will more accurately represent how much of an asset's usefulness is being used up each year. For tax purposes, accelerated depreciation provides a way of deferring corporate income taxes by reducing taxable income in current years, in exchange for increased taxable income in future years.
Accounts receivable	Accounts receivable is money owed to a business by its clients (customers or debtors) and shown on its balance sheet as an asset. It is one of a series of accounting transactions dealing with the billing of a customer for goods and services that the customer has ordered. Overview Accounts receivable represents money owed by entities to the firm on the sale of products or services on credit.
Quick ratio	In finance, the Acid-test or quick ratio or liquid ratio measures the ability of a company to use its near cash or quick assets to extinguish or retire its current liabilities immediately. Quick assets include those current assets that presumably can be quickly converted to cash at close to their book values. A company with a Quick Ratio of less than 1 cannot currently pay back its current liabilities.
Inventory turnover	In accounting, the Inventory turnover is a measure of the number of times inventory is sold or used in a time period such as a year. The equation for inventory turnover equals the cost of goods sold divided by the average inventory. Inventory turnover is also known as inventory turns, stockturn, stock turns, turns, and stock turnover.
Days sales outstanding	In accountancy, days sales outstanding is a calculation used by a company to estimate their average collection period. It is a financial ratio that illustrates how well a company's accounts receivables are being managed. The days sales outstanding figure is an index of the relationship between outstanding receivables and credit account sales achieved over a given period.
Net profit margin	Profit margin, net margin, net profit margin or net profit ratio all refer to a measure of profitability. It is calculated by finding the net profit as a percentage of the revenue. $$\text{Net profit Margin} = \frac{\text{Net Profit}}{\text{Revenue}}$$ where Net Profit = Revenue - Cost profit percentage is calculated with cost price taken as base.
Operating margin	In business, operating margin - also known as operating income margin, operating profit margin and return on sales (ROS) - is the ratio of operating income ('operating profit' in the UK) divided by net sales, usually presented in percent.

Visit Cram101.com for full Practice Exams

8. Stock

CHAPTER HIGHLIGHTS & NOTES: KEY TERMS, PEOPLE, PLACES, CONCEPTS

$$\text{Operating margin} = \left(\frac{\text{Operating income}}{\text{Revenue}}\right)$$

Net profit measures the profitability of ventures after accounting for all costs.

Return on sales (ROS) is net profit as a percentage of sales revenue.

Return on assets	The return on assets percentage shows how profitable a company's assets are in generating revenue.
	Return on assets can be computed as:
	This number tells you what the company can do with what it has, i.e. how many dollars of earnings they derive from each dollar of assets they control. It's a useful number for comparing competing companies in the same industry.
Return on equity	Return on equity measures the rate of return on the ownership interest (shareholders' equity) of the common stock owners. It measures a firm's efficiency at generating profits from every unit of shareholders' equity (also known as net assets or assets minus liabilities). Return on equity shows how well a company uses investment funds to generate earnings growth.
Debt-to-equity ratio	The debt-to-equity ratio is a financial ratio indicating the relative proportion of shareholders' equity and debt used to finance a company's assets. Closely related to leveraging, the ratio is also known as Risk, Gearing or Leverage. The two components are often taken from the firm's balance sheet or statement of financial position (so-called book value), but the ratio may also be calculated using market values for both, if the company's debt and equity are publicly traded, or using a combination of book value for debt and market value for equity financially.
Financial risk	Financial risk is an umbrella term for multiple types of risk associated with financing, including financial transactions that include company loans in risk of default. Risk is a term often used to imply downside risk, meaning the uncertainty of a return and the potential for financial loss.
	A science has evolved around managing market and financial risk under the general title of modern portfolio theory initiated by Dr. Harry Markowitz in 1952 with his article, 'Portfolio Selection'.
Debt ratio	Debt Ratio is a financial ratio that indicates the percentage of a company's assets that are provided via debt. It is the ratio of total debt (the sum of current liabilities and long-term liabilities) and total assets (the sum of current assets, fixed assets, and other assets such as 'goodwill').

$$\text{Debt ratio} = \frac{\text{Total Debt}}{\text{Total Assets}}$$

Visit Cram101.com for full Practice Exams

8. Stock

CHAPTER HIGHLIGHTS & NOTES: KEY TERMS, PEOPLE, PLACES, CONCEPTS

or alternatively:

$$\text{Debt ratio} = \frac{\text{Total Liability}}{\text{Total Assets}}$$

For example, a company with $2 million in total assets and $500,000 in total liabilities would have a debt ratio of 25%.

Cash flow statement | In financial accounting, a cash flow statement, is a financial statement that shows how changes in balance sheet accounts and income affect cash and cash equivalents, and breaks the analysis down to operating, investing, and financing activities. Essentially, the cash flow statement is concerned with the flow of cash in and out of the business. The statement captures both the current operating results and the accompanying changes in the balance sheet.

CHAPTER QUIZ: KEY TERMS, PEOPLE, PLACES, CONCEPTS

1. _____s are payments made by a corporation to its shareholder members. It is the portion of corporate profits paid out to stockholders. When a corporation earns a profit or surplus, that money can be put to two uses: it can either be re-invested in the business (called retained earnings), or it can be distributed to shareholders.

    a. Bonus share
    b. Common stock dividend
    c. Dividend
    d. Dividend cover

2. A _____ is a body of elected or appointed members who jointly oversee the activities of a company or organization. Other names include board of governors, board of managers, board of regents, board of trustees, and board of visitors. It is often simply referred to as 'the board'.

    a. Board of directors
    b. Companies Acts
    c. Complex structured finance transactions
    d. Doing business as

3. . _____ is a multiple-winner voting system intended to promote more proportional representation than winner-take-all elections.

8. Stock

CHAPTER QUIZ: KEY TERMS, PEOPLE, PLACES, CONCEPTS

_____ is used frequently in corporate governance, where it is mandated by some (7) U.S. states. It was used to elect the Illinois House of Representatives from 1870 until its repeal in 1980 and used in England in the late 19th century to elect some school boards.

- a. granularity
- b. Cumulative voting
- c. Public float
- d. Public offering

4. A _____ is a legal document relating to the formation of a company or corporation. It is a license to form a corporation issued by state government. Its precise meaning depends upon the legal system in which it is used, but the two primary meanings are: Commonwealth systems

   In the U.S.A. a _____ is usually used as an alternative description of a corporation's articles of incorporation.

   - a. Certificate of incorporation
   - b. Companies law
   - c. Company mortgage
   - d. Consignment agreement

5. _____ is an umbrella term for multiple types of risk associated with financing, including financial transactions that include company loans in risk of default. Risk is a term often used to imply downside risk, meaning the uncertainty of a return and the potential for financial loss.

   A science has evolved around managing market and _____ under the general title of modern portfolio theory initiated by Dr. Harry Markowitz in 1952 with his article, 'Portfolio Selection'.

   - a. Financial transaction
   - b. Forecast period
   - c. Future-oriented
   - d. Financial risk

Visit Cram101.com for full Practice Exams

ANSWER KEY
8. Stock

1. c
2. a
3. b
4. a
5. d

You can take the complete Chapter Practice Test

for 8. Stock
on all key terms, persons, places, and concepts.

Online 99 Cents

http://www.epub2174.13.22362.8.cram101.com/

Use www.Cram101.com for all your study needs

including Cram101's online interactive problem solving labs in

chemistry, statistics, mathematics, and more.

9. The Valuation of Common Stock

CHAPTER OUTLINE: KEY TERMS, PEOPLE, PLACES, CONCEPTS

- Financial planning
- Capital gain
- Expected return
- Return on assets
- Return on equity
- Common stock
- Valuation
- Stock valuation
- Capital asset pricing model
- Security market line
- Cash flow
- Quantitative fund
- Book value
- PEG ratio
- Profit margin
- Growth investing
- Event study

Visit Cram101.com for full Practice Exams

9. The Valuation of Common Stock

CHAPTER HIGHLIGHTS & NOTES: KEY TERMS, PEOPLE, PLACES, CONCEPTS

Financial planning	Financial planning is the task of determining how a business will afford to achieve its strategic goals and objectives. Usually, a company creates a Financial Plan immediately after the vision and objectives have been set. The Financial Plan describes each of the activities, resources, equipment and materials that are needed to achieve these objectives, as well as the timeframes involved.
Capital gain	A capital gain is a profit that results from a disposition of a capital asset, such as stock, bond or real estate, where the amount realized on the disposition exceeds the purchase price. The gain is the difference between a higher selling price and a lower purchase price. Conversely, a capital loss arises if the proceeds from the sale of a capital asset are less than the purchase price.
Expected return	The expected return is the expected value of a random variable usually representing a gain, i.e. the weighted-average outcome in gambling, probability theory, economics or finance. It is calculated by using the following formula: How do you calculate the average of a probability distribution? As denoted by the above formula, simply take the probability of each possible return outcome and multiply it by the return outcome itself. For example, if you knew a given investment had a 50% chance of earning a 10 return, a 25% chance of earning 20 and a 25% chance of earning -10, the expected return would be equal to 7.5: Although this is what you expect the return to be, there is no guarantee that it will be the actual return.
Return on assets	The return on assets percentage shows how profitable a company's assets are in generating revenue. Return on assets can be computed as: This number tells you what the company can do with what it has, i.e. how many dollars of earnings they derive from each dollar of assets they control. It's a useful number for comparing competing companies in the same industry.
Return on equity	Return on equity measures the rate of return on the ownership interest (shareholders' equity) of the common stock owners. It measures a firm's efficiency at generating profits from every unit of shareholders' equity (also known as net assets or assets minus liabilities). Return on equity shows how well a company uses investment funds to generate earnings growth.
Common stock	Common stock is a form of corporate equity ownership, a type of security. The terms 'voting share' or 'ordinary share' are also used in other parts of the world; common stock being primarily used in the United States.

Visit Cram101.com for full Practice Exams

9. The Valuation of Common Stock

CHAPTER HIGHLIGHTS & NOTES: KEY TERMS, PEOPLE, PLACES, CONCEPTS

Valuation	In finance, valuation is the process of estimating what something is worth. Items that are usually valued are a financial asset or liability. Valuations can be done on assets (for example, investments in marketable securities such as stocks, options, business enterprises, or intangible assets such as patents and trademarks) or on liabilities (e.g., bonds issued by a company).
Stock valuation	In financial markets, stock valuation is the method of calculating theoretical values of companies and their stocks. The main use of these methods is to predict future market prices, or more generally, potential market prices, and thus to profit from price movement - stocks that are judged undervalued (with respect to their theoretical value) are bought, while stocks that are judged overvalued are sold, in the expectation that undervalued stocks will, on the whole, rise in value, while overvalued stocks will, on the whole, fall. In the view of fundamental analysis, stock valuation based on fundamentals aims to give an estimate of their intrinsic value of the stock, based on predictions of the future cash flows and profitability of the business.
Capital asset pricing model	In finance, the capital asset pricing model is used to determine a theoretically appropriate required rate of return of an asset, if that asset is to be added to an already well-diversified portfolio, given that asset's non-diversifiable risk. The model takes into account the asset's sensitivity to non-diversifiable risk (also known as systematic risk or market risk), often represented by the quantity beta (β) in the financial industry, as well as the expected return of the market and the expected return of a theoretical risk-free asset. The model was introduced by Jack Treynor (1961, 1962), William Sharpe (1964), John Lintner (1965a,b) and Jan Mossin (1966) independently, building on the earlier work of Harry Markowitz on diversification and modern portfolio theory.
Security market line	Security market line is the representation of the Capital asset pricing model. It displays the expected rate of return of an individual security as a function of systematic, non-diversifiable risk (its beta). Formula The Y-intercept of the security market line is equal to the risk-free interest rate. The slope of the Security market line is equal to the market risk premium and reflects the risk return trade off at a given time: $\mathrm{SML}: E(R_i) = R_f + \beta_i[E(R_M) - R_f]$
Cash flow	Cash flow is the movement of money into or out of a business, project, or financial product. It is usually measured during a specified, finite period of time. Measurement of cash flow can be used for calculating other parameters that give information on a company's value and situation.
Quantitative fund	A quantitative fund are determined by numerical methods rather than by human judgement.

9. The Valuation of Common Stock

CHAPTER HIGHLIGHTS & NOTES: KEY TERMS, PEOPLE, PLACES, CONCEPTS

	In recent years, quantitatively managed funds have become a fashionable way for newly launched mutual funds. The tide rushed through the whole North America as more and more asset managers adopted statistical models to explore alphas that hide behind the market abnormalities.
Book value	In accounting, book value is the value of an asset according to its balance sheet account balance. For assets, the value is based on the original cost of the asset less any depreciation, amortization or Impairment costs made against the asset. Traditionally, a company's book value is its total assets minus intangible assets and liabilities.
PEG ratio	The PEG ratio is a valuation metric for determining the relative trade-off between the price of a stock, the earnings generated per share (EPS), and the company's expected growth. In general, the P/E ratio is higher for a company with a higher growth rate. Thus using just the P/E ratio would make high-growth companies appear overvalued relative to others.
Profit margin	Profit margin, net margin, net profit margin or net profit ratio all refer to a measure of profitability. It is calculated by finding the net profit as a percentage of the revenue. $$\text{Net profit Margin} = \frac{\text{Net Profit}}{\text{Revenue}}$$ where Net Profit = Revenue - Cost profit percentage is calculated with cost price taken as base.
Growth investing	Growth investing is a style of investment strategy. Those who follow this style, known as growth investors, invest in companies that exhibit signs of above-average growth, even if the share price appears expensive in terms of metrics such as price-to-earnings or price-to-book ratios. In typical usage, the term 'growth investing' contrasts with the strategy known as value investing.
Event study	An Event study is a statistical method to assess the impact of an event on the value of a firm. The basic idea is to find the abnormal return attributable to the event being studied by adjusting for the return that stems from the price fluctuation of the market as a whole. As the event methodology can be used to elicit the effects of any type of event on the direction and magnitude of stock price changes, it is very versatile.

Visit Cram101.com for full Practice Exams

9. The Valuation of Common Stock

CHAPTER QUIZ: KEY TERMS, PEOPLE, PLACES, CONCEPTS

1. _____ is a form of corporate equity ownership, a type of security. The terms 'voting share' or 'ordinary share' are also used in other parts of the world; _____ being primarily used in the United States.

    It is called 'common' to distinguish it from preferred stock.

    a. Common stock
    b. Control premium
    c. Corporate synergy
    d. Critical accounting policy

2. In finance, _____ is the process of estimating what something is worth. Items that are usually valued are a financial asset or liability. _____s can be done on assets (for example, investments in marketable securities such as stocks, options, business enterprises, or intangible assets such as patents and trademarks) or on liabilities (e.g., bonds issued by a company).

    a. Value investing
    b. Virtual bidding
    c. Valuation
    d. Yellow strip

3. _____ is the representation of the Capital asset pricing model. It displays the expected rate of return of an individual security as a function of systematic, non-diversifiable risk (its beta). Formula

    The Y-intercept of the _____ is equal to the risk-free interest rate. The slope of the _____ is equal to the market risk premium and reflects the risk return trade off at a given time:
    $$SML : E(R_i) = R_f + \beta_i[E(R_M) - R_f]$$

    a. Benchmark-driven investment strategy
    b. Benefits realisation management
    c. Binary option
    d. Security market line

4. The _____ percentage shows how profitable a company's assets are in generating revenue.

    _____ can be computed as:

    This number tells you what the company can do with what it has, i.e. how many dollars of earnings they derive from each dollar of assets they control. It's a useful number for comparing competing companies in the same industry.

    a. Return on net assets
    b. Electronic Data-Gathering, Analysis, and Retrieval system
    c. Return on assets
    d. Inclusion-exclusion principle

9. The Valuation of Common Stock

CHAPTER QUIZ: KEY TERMS, PEOPLE, PLACES, CONCEPTS

5. The _____ is the expected value of a random variable usually representing a gain, i.e. the weighted-average outcome in gambling, probability theory, economics or finance.

   It is calculated by using the following formula:

   How do you calculate the average of a probability distribution? As denoted by the above formula, simply take the probability of each possible return outcome and multiply it by the return outcome itself. For example, if you knew a given investment had a 50% chance of earning a 10 return, a 25% chance of earning 20 and a 25% chance of earning -10, the _____ would be equal to 7.5:

   Although this is what you expect the return to be, there is no guarantee that it will be the actual return.

   a. Experiment
   b. Impossibility of a gambling system
   c. Expected return
   d. Inclusion-exclusion principle

ANSWER KEY
9. The Valuation of Common Stock

1. a
2. c
3. d
4. c
5. c

You can take the complete Chapter Practice Test

for 9. The Valuation of Common Stock
on all key terms, persons, places, and concepts.

Online 99 Cents

http://www.epub2174.13.22362.9.cram101.com/

Use www.Cram101.com for all your study needs

including Cram101's online interactive problem solving labs in

chemistry, statistics, mathematics, and more.

10. Investment Returns and Aggregate Measures of Stock Markets

CHAPTER OUTLINE: KEY TERMS, PEOPLE, PLACES, CONCEPTS

- Stock index
- Stock split
- American depositary receipt
- NYSE Composite
- Real estate investment trust
- Exchange-traded fund
- Holding period return
- Common stock
- Internal rate of return
- Rate of return
- Yield to maturity
- Standard deviation
- Capital asset pricing model
- Dollar cost averaging
- Cumulative voting
- Dividend reinvestment plan

10. Investment Returns and Aggregate Measures of Stock Markets

CHAPTER HIGHLIGHTS & NOTES: KEY TERMS, PEOPLE, PLACES, CONCEPTS

Stock index	A stock index is a method of measuring the value of a section of the stock market. It is computed from the prices of selected stocks (sometimes a weighted average). It is a tool used by investors and financial managers to describe the market, and to compare the return on specific investments.
Stock split	A stock split or stock divide increases the number of shares in a public company. The price is adjusted such that the before and after market capitalization of the company remains the same and dilution does not occur. Options and warrants are included.
American depositary receipt	An American depositary receipt is a negotiable security that represents securities of a non-US company that trade in the US financial markets. Securities of a foreign company that are represented by an American depositary receipt are called American depositary shares (ADSs). Shares of many non-US companies trade on US stock exchanges through American depositary receipts.
NYSE Composite	The NYSE Composite is a stock market index covering all common stock listed on the New York Stock Exchange, including American Depositary Receipts, Real Estate Investment Trusts, tracking stocks, and foreign listings. Over 2,000 stocks are covered in the index, of which over 1,600 are from United States corporations and over 360 are foreign listings; however foreign companies are very prevalent among the largest companies in the index: of the 100 companies in the index having the largest market capitalization (and thus the largest impact on the index), more than half (55) are non-U.S. issues. This includes corporations in each of the ten industries listed in the Industry Classification Benchmark.
Real estate investment trust	A real estate investment trust is a tax designation for a corporate entity investing in real estate. The purpose of this designation is to reduce or eliminate corporate tax. In return, Real estate investment trusts are required to distribute at least 90% of their taxable income into the hands of investors.
Exchange-traded fund	An exchange-traded fund is an investment fund traded on stock exchanges, much like stocks. An ETF holds assets such as stocks, commodities, or bonds, and trades close to its net asset value over the course of the trading day. Most ETFs track an index, such as the S&P 500 or MSCI EAFE. ETFs may be attractive as investments because of their low costs, tax efficiency, and stock-like features.
Holding period return	In finance, holding period return is the total return on an asset or portfolio over the period during which it was held. It is one of the simplest measures of investment performance. Holding period return is the percentage by which the value of a portfolio has grown for a particular period.
Common stock	Common stock is a form of corporate equity ownership, a type of security.

Visit Cram101.com for full Practice Exams

10. Investment Returns and Aggregate Measures of Stock Markets

CHAPTER HIGHLIGHTS & NOTES: KEY TERMS, PEOPLE, PLACES, CONCEPTS

	The terms 'voting share' or 'ordinary share' are also used in other parts of the world; common stock being primarily used in the United States. It is called 'common' to distinguish it from preferred stock.
Internal rate of return	The internal rate of return or economic rate of return (ERR) is a rate of return used in capital budgeting to measure and compare the profitability of investments. It is also called the discounted cash flow rate of return (DCFROR) or the rate of return (ROR). In the context of savings and loans the IRR is also called the effective interest rate.
Rate of return	In finance, rate of return also known as return on investment (ROI), rate of profit or sometimes just return, is the ratio of money gained or lost (whether realized or unrealized) on an investment relative to the amount of money invested. The amount of money gained or lost may be referred to as interest, profit/loss, gain/loss, or net income/loss. The money invested may be referred to as the asset, capital, principal, or the cost basis of the investment.
Yield to maturity	The Yield to maturity or redemption yield of a bond or other fixed-interest security, such as gilts, is the internal rate of return (IRR, overall interest rate) earned by an investor who buys the bond today at the market price, assuming that the bond will be held until maturity, and that all coupon and principal payments will be made on schedule. Contrary to popular belief, including concepts often cited in advanced financial literature, Yield to maturity does NOT depend upon a reinvestment of coupon payments. Yield to maturity, rather, is simply the discount rate at which the sum of all future cash flows from the bond (coupons and principal) is equal to the price of the bond.
Standard deviation	In statistics and probability theory, standard deviation shows how much variation or 'dispersion' exists from the average (mean, or expected value).A low standard deviation indicates that the data points tend to be very close to the mean.High standard deviation indicates that the data points are spread out over a large range of values. The standard deviation of a random variable, statistical population, data set, or probability distribution is the square root of its variance. It is algebraically simpler though practically less robust than the average absolute deviation.
Capital asset pricing model	In finance, the capital asset pricing model is used to determine a theoretically appropriate required rate of return of an asset, if that asset is to be added to an already well-diversified portfolio, given that asset's non-diversifiable risk. The model takes into account the asset's sensitivity to non-diversifiable risk (also known as systematic risk or market risk), often represented by the quantity beta (β) in the financial industry, as well as the expected return of the market and the expected return of a theoretical risk-free asset.

10. Investment Returns and Aggregate Measures of Stock Markets

CHAPTER HIGHLIGHTS & NOTES: KEY TERMS, PEOPLE, PLACES, CONCEPTS

Dollar cost averaging	Dollar cost averaging is an investment strategy that may be used with any currency. It takes the form of investing equal monetary amounts regularly and periodically over specific time periods (such as $100 monthly for 10 months) in a particular investment or portfolio. By doing so, more shares are purchased when prices are low and fewer shares are purchased when prices are high.
Cumulative voting	Cumulative voting is a multiple-winner voting system intended to promote more proportional representation than winner-take-all elections. Cumulative voting is used frequently in corporate governance, where it is mandated by some (7) U.S. states. It was used to elect the Illinois House of Representatives from 1870 until its repeal in 1980 and used in England in the late 19th century to elect some school boards.
Dividend reinvestment plan	A dividend reinvestment program or dividend reinvestment plan is an equity investment option offered directly from the underlying company. The investor does not receive quarterly dividends directly as cash; instead, the investor's dividends are directly reinvested in the underlying equity. (The investor must still pay tax annually on his or her dividend income, whether it is received or reinvested).

CHAPTER QUIZ: KEY TERMS, PEOPLE, PLACES, CONCEPTS

1. In statistics and probability theory, _____ shows how much variation or 'dispersion' exists from the average (mean, or expected value).A low _____ indicates that the data points tend to be very close to the mean.High _____ indicates that the data points are spread out over a large range of values.

   The _____ of a random variable, statistical population, data set, or probability distribution is the square root of its variance. It is algebraically simpler though practically less robust than the average absolute deviation.

   a. Percentile
   b. Standard deviation
   c. Quartile
   d. frequency distribution

2. . An _____ is a negotiable security that represents securities of a non-US company that trade in the US financial markets. Securities of a foreign company that are represented by an _____ are called American depositary shares (ADSs).

   Shares of many non-US companies trade on US stock exchanges through _____s.

   a. At the opening
   b. Avanza

Visit Cram101.com for full Practice Exams

10. Investment Returns and Aggregate Measures of Stock Markets

CHAPTER QUIZ: KEY TERMS, PEOPLE, PLACES, CONCEPTS

    c. Employee stock option
    d. American depositary receipt

3. The _____ or economic rate of return (ERR) is a rate of return used in capital budgeting to measure and compare the profitability of investments. It is also called the discounted cash flow rate of return (DCFROR) or the rate of return (ROR). In the context of savings and loans the IRR is also called the effective interest rate.

    a. OpenIPO
    b. Operating ratio
    c. Underwriting contract
    d. Internal rate of return

4. In finance, _____ is the total return on an asset or portfolio over the period during which it was held. It is one of the simplest measures of investment performance.

    _____ is the percentage by which the value of a portfolio has grown for a particular period.

    a. Ho-Lee model
    b. Hull-White model
    c. Jamshidian's trick
    d. Holding period return

5. The _____ is a stock market index covering all common stock listed on the New York Stock Exchange, including American Depositary Receipts, Real Estate Investment Trusts, tracking stocks, and foreign listings. Over 2,000 stocks are covered in the index, of which over 1,600 are from United States corporations and over 360 are foreign listings; however foreign companies are very prevalent among the largest companies in the index: of the 100 companies in the index having the largest market capitalization (and thus the largest impact on the index), more than half (55) are non-U.S. issues. This includes corporations in each of the ten industries listed in the Industry Classification Benchmark.

    a. Russell index
    b. granularity
    c. Jimmy Carter
    d. NYSE Composite

Visit Cram101.com for full Practice Exams

ANSWER KEY
10. Investment Returns and Aggregate Measures of Stock Markets

1. b
2. d
3. d
4. d
5. d

You can take the complete Chapter Practice Test

for 10. Investment Returns and Aggregate Measures of Stock Markets
on all key terms, persons, places, and concepts.

Online 99 Cents

http://www.epub2174.13.22362.10.cram101.com/

Use www.Cram101.com for all your study needs

including Cram101's online interactive problem solving labs in

chemistry, statistics, mathematics, and more.

11. The Macroeconomic Environment for Investment Decisions

CHAPTER OUTLINE: KEY TERMS, PEOPLE, PLACES, CONCEPTS

	Business cycle
	Commercial bank
	Gross domestic product
	Fiscal policy
	Monetary policy
	Consumer Confidence Index
	Consumer price index
	Producer price index
	Deflation
	Financial risk
	Term structure
	Discount rate
	Excess reserves
	Federal funds rate
	Reserve requirement
	Forward contract
	Open market operation
	Capital asset pricing model
	Money supply
	Deficit spending

Visit Cram101.com for full Practice Exams

11. The Macroeconomic Environment for Investment Decisions

CHAPTER HIGHLIGHTS & NOTES: KEY TERMS, PEOPLE, PLACES, CONCEPTS

Business cycle	The term business cycle refers to economy-wide fluctuations in production, trade and economic activity in general over several months or years in an economy organized on free-enterprise principles. These fluctuations occur around a long-term growth trend, and typically involve shifts over time between periods of relatively rapid economic growth (an expansion or boom), and periods of relative stagnation or decline (a contraction or recession). Business cycles are usually measured by considering the growth rate of real gross domestic product.
Commercial bank	A commercial bank is a type of financial institution and intermediary. It is a bank that provides transactional, savings, and money market accounts and that accepts time deposits. After the implementation of the Glass-Steagall Act, the U.S. Congress required that banks engage only in banking activities, whereas investment banks were limited to capital market activities.
Gross domestic product	Gross domestic product refers to the market value of all officially recognized final goods and services produced within a country in a given period. Gross domestic product per capita is often considered an indicator of a country's standard of living; Gross domestic product per capita is not a measure of personal income. Under economic theory, Gross domestic product per capita exactly equals the gross domestic income (GDI) per capita.
Fiscal policy	In economics and political science, fiscal policy is the use of government revenue collection (taxation) and expenditure (spending) to influence the economy. The two main instruments of fiscal policy are government taxation and changes in the level and composition of taxation and government spending can affect the following variables in the economy:•Aggregate demand and the level of economic activity;•The distribution of income;•The pattern of resource allocation within the government sector and relative to the private sector Fiscal policy refers to the use of the government budget to influence economic activity. Stances of fiscal policy The three main stances of fiscal policy are:•Neutral fiscal policy is usually undertaken when an economy is in equilibrium.
Monetary policy	Monetary policy is the process by which the monetary authority of a country control the supply of money, often targeting a rate of interest for the purpose of promoting economic growth and stability. The official goals usually include relatively stable prices and low unemployment. Monetary theory provides insight into how to craft optimal monetary policy.
Consumer Confidence Index	The U.S. Consumer Confidence Index is an indicator designed to measure consumer confidence, which is defined as the degree of optimism on the state of the economy that consumers are expressing through their activities of savings and spending.

11. The Macroeconomic Environment for Investment Decisions

CHAPTER HIGHLIGHTS & NOTES: KEY TERMS, PEOPLE, PLACES, CONCEPTS

	Global consumer confidence is not measured. Country by country analysis indicates huge variance around the globe.
Consumer price index	A consumer price index measures changes in the price level of consumer goods and services purchased by households. The Consumer price index is defined by the United States Bureau of Labor Statistics as 'a measure of the average change over time in the prices paid by urban consumers for a market basket of consumer goods and services.'
	The Consumer price index is a statistical estimate constructed using the prices of a sample of representative items whose prices are collected periodically. Sub-indexes and sub-sub-indexes are computed for different categories and sub-categories of goods and services, being combined to produce the overall index with weights reflecting their shares in the total of the consumer expenditures covered by the index.
Producer price index	A Producer Price Index measures average changes in prices received by domestic producers for their output. It is one of several price indices.
	Its importance is being undermined by the steady decline in manufactured goods as a share of spending.
Deflation	In economics, deflation is a decrease in the general price level of goods and services. Deflation occurs when the inflation rate falls below 0% (a negative inflation rate). This should not be confused with disinflation, a slow-down in the inflation rate (i.e. when inflation declines to lower levels).
Financial risk	Financial risk is an umbrella term for multiple types of risk associated with financing, including financial transactions that include company loans in risk of default. Risk is a term often used to imply downside risk, meaning the uncertainty of a return and the potential for financial loss.
	A science has evolved around managing market and financial risk under the general title of modern portfolio theory initiated by Dr. Harry Markowitz in 1952 with his article, 'Portfolio Selection'.
Term structure	In finance, the yield curve is a curve showing several yields or interest rates across different contract lengths for a similar debt contract. The curve shows the relation between the (level of) interest rate (or cost of borrowing) and the time to maturity, known as the 'term', of the debt for a given borrower in a given currency. For example, the U.S. dollar interest rates paid on U.S. Treasury securities for various maturities are closely watched by many traders, and are commonly plotted on a graph such as the one on the right which is informally called 'the yield curve.' More formal mathematical descriptions of this relation are often called the term structure of interest rates.

11. The Macroeconomic Environment for Investment Decisions

CHAPTER HIGHLIGHTS & NOTES: KEY TERMS, PEOPLE, PLACES, CONCEPTS

Discount rate	The discount rate can mean·an interest rate a central bank charges depository institutions that borrow reserves from it, for example for the use of the Federal Reserve's discount window·the same as interest rate; the term 'discount' does not refer to the common meaning of the word, but to the meaning in computations of present value, e.g. net present value or discounted cash flow·the annual effective discount rate, which is the annual interest divided by the capital including that interest; this rate is lower than the interest rate; it corresponds to using the value after a year as the nominal value, and seeing the initial value as the nominal value minus a discount; it is used for Treasury Bills and similar financial instrumentsAnnual effective discount rate The annual effective discount rate is the annual interest divided by the capital including that interest, which is the interest rate divided by 100% plus the interest rate. It is the annual discount factor to be applied to the future cash flow, to find the discount, subtracted from a future value to find the value one year earlier. For example, suppose there is a government bond that sells for $95 and pays $100 in a year's time.
Excess reserves	In banking, excess reserves are bank reserves in excess of the reserve requirement set by a central bank. They are reserves of cash more than the required amounts. Holding excess reserves has an opportunity cost if higher risk-adjusted interest can be earned by putting the funds elsewhere; the advantage of holding some funds in excess reserves is that doing so may provide enhanced liquidity and therefore more smooth operation of payment system.
Federal funds rate	In the United States, the federal funds rate is the interest rate at which depository institutions actively trade balances held at the Federal Reserve, called federal funds, with each other, usually overnight, on an uncollateralized basis. Institutions with surplus balances in their accounts lend those balances to institutions in need of larger balances. The federal funds rate is an important benchmark in financial markets.
Reserve requirement	The reserve requirement is a central bank regulation that sets the minimum fraction of customer deposits and notes that each commercial bank must hold as reserves (rather than lend out). These required reserves are normally in the form of cash stored physically in a bank vault (vault cash) or deposits made with a central bank. The required reserve ratio is sometimes used as a tool in monetary policy, influencing the country's borrowing and interest rates by changing the amount of funds available for banks to make loans with.
Forward contract	In finance, a forward contract is a non-standardized contract between two parties to buy or sell an asset at a specified future time at a price agreed upon today. This is in contrast to a spot contract, which is an agreement to buy or sell an asset today.

11. The Macroeconomic Environment for Investment Decisions

CHAPTER HIGHLIGHTS & NOTES: KEY TERMS, PEOPLE, PLACES, CONCEPTS

Open market operation	An open market operation is an activity by a central bank to buy or sell government bonds on the open market. A central bank uses them as the primary means of implementing monetary policy. The usual aim of open market operations is to manipulate the short term interest rate and the supply of base money in an economy, and thus indirectly control the total money supply.
Capital asset pricing model	In finance, the capital asset pricing model is used to determine a theoretically appropriate required rate of return of an asset, if that asset is to be added to an already well-diversified portfolio, given that asset's non-diversifiable risk. The model takes into account the asset's sensitivity to non-diversifiable risk (also known as systematic risk or market risk), often represented by the quantity beta (β) in the financial industry, as well as the expected return of the market and the expected return of a theoretical risk-free asset. The model was introduced by Jack Treynor (1961, 1962), William Sharpe (1964), John Lintner (1965a,b) and Jan Mossin (1966) independently, building on the earlier work of Harry Markowitz on diversification and modern portfolio theory.
Money supply	In economics, the money supply, is the total amount of monetary assets available in an economy at a specific time. There are several ways to define 'money,' but standard measures usually include currency in circulation and demand deposits (depositors' easily accessed assets on the books of financial institutions). Money supply data are recorded and published, usually by the government or the central bank of the country.
Deficit spending	Deficit spending is the amount by which spending exceeds revenue over a particular period of time, also called simply deficit, or budget deficit; the opposite of budget surplus. The term may be applied to the budget of a government, private company, or individual. Government deficit spending is a central point of controversy in economics, as discussed below.

11. The Macroeconomic Environment for Investment Decisions

CHAPTER QUIZ: KEY TERMS, PEOPLE, PLACES, CONCEPTS

1. In finance, the _____ is used to determine a theoretically appropriate required rate of return of an asset, if that asset is to be added to an already well-diversified portfolio, given that asset's non-diversifiable risk. The model takes into account the asset's sensitivity to non-diversifiable risk (also known as systematic risk or market risk), often represented by the quantity beta (β) in the financial industry, as well as the expected return of the market and the expected return of a theoretical risk-free asset.

   The model was introduced by Jack Treynor (1961, 1962), William Sharpe (1964), John Lintner (1965a,b) and Jan Mossin (1966) independently, building on the earlier work of Harry Markowitz on diversification and modern portfolio theory.

   a. Capital asset pricing model
   b. Chen model
   c. Chepakovich valuation model
   d. Constant elasticity of variance model

2. In banking, _____ are bank reserves in excess of the reserve requirement set by a central bank. They are reserves of cash more than the required amounts. Holding _____ has an opportunity cost if higher risk-adjusted interest can be earned by putting the funds elsewhere; the advantage of holding some funds in _____ is that doing so may provide enhanced liquidity and therefore more smooth operation of payment system.

   a. Excess reserves
   b. Financial export
   c. Financial innovation
   d. Financial literacy

3. _____ refers to the market value of all officially recognized final goods and services produced within a country in a given period. _____ per capita is often considered an indicator of a country's standard of living; _____ per capita is not a measure of personal income. Under economic theory, _____ per capita exactly equals the gross domestic income (GDI) per capita.

   a. capital formation
   b. Wesley Clair Mitchell
   c. Gross domestic product
   d. Skyscraper Index

4. . A _____ is a type of financial institution and intermediary. It is a bank that provides transactional, savings, and money market accounts and that accepts time deposits.

   After the implementation of the Glass-Steagall Act, the U.S. Congress required that banks engage only in banking activities, whereas investment banks were limited to capital market activities.

   a. Community development bank
   b. Wesley Clair Mitchell
   c. Reference date

Visit Cram101.com for full Practice Exams

11. The Macroeconomic Environment for Investment Decisions

CHAPTER QUIZ: KEY TERMS, PEOPLE, PLACES, CONCEPTS

5. A _____ measures changes in the price level of consumer goods and services purchased by households. The _____ is defined by the United States Bureau of Labor Statistics as 'a measure of the average change over time in the prices paid by urban consumers for a market basket of consumer goods and services.'

The _____ is a statistical estimate constructed using the prices of a sample of representative items whose prices are collected periodically. Sub-indexes and sub-sub-indexes are computed for different categories and sub-categories of goods and services, being combined to produce the overall index with weights reflecting their shares in the total of the consumer expenditures covered by the index.

a. Higher Education Price Index
b. Consumer price index
c. Chicago plan
d. Contractionary monetary policy

ANSWER KEY
11. The Macroeconomic Environment for Investment Decisions

1. a
2. a
3. c
4. d
5. b

You can take the complete Chapter Practice Test

for 11. The Macroeconomic Environment for Investment Decisions
on all key terms, persons, places, and concepts.

Online 99 Cents

http://www.epub2174.13.22362.11.cram101.com/

Use www.Cram101.com for all your study needs

including Cram101's online interactive problem solving labs in

chemistry, statistics, mathematics, and more.

12. Behavioral Finance and Technical Analysis

CHAPTER OUTLINE: KEY TERMS, PEOPLE, PLACES, CONCEPTS

- Behavioral Finance
- Capital asset pricing model
- Capital gain
- Disposition effect
- Ostrich effect
- Cognitive dissonance
- Adaptive market hypothesis
- Book value
- Contrarian
- Stock valuation
- Dow theory
- Bar chart
- Moving average
- Oscillator
- Technical analysis
- Diversification

Visit Cram101.com for full Practice Exams

12. Behavioral Finance and Technical Analysis

CHAPTER HIGHLIGHTS & NOTES: KEY TERMS, PEOPLE, PLACES, CONCEPTS

Behavioral Finance	Behavioral economics and the related field, behavioral finance, study the effects of social, cognitive, and emotional factors on the economic decisions of individuals and institutions and the consequences for market prices, returns, and the resource allocation. The fields are primarily concerned with the bounds of rationality of economic agents. Behavioral models typically integrate insights from psychology with neo-classical economic theory.
Capital asset pricing model	In finance, the capital asset pricing model is used to determine a theoretically appropriate required rate of return of an asset, if that asset is to be added to an already well-diversified portfolio, given that asset's non-diversifiable risk. The model takes into account the asset's sensitivity to non-diversifiable risk (also known as systematic risk or market risk), often represented by the quantity beta (β) in the financial industry, as well as the expected return of the market and the expected return of a theoretical risk-free asset. The model was introduced by Jack Treynor (1961, 1962), William Sharpe (1964), John Lintner (1965a,b) and Jan Mossin (1966) independently, building on the earlier work of Harry Markowitz on diversification and modern portfolio theory.
Capital gain	A capital gain is a profit that results from a disposition of a capital asset, such as stock, bond or real estate, where the amount realized on the disposition exceeds the purchase price. The gain is the difference between a higher selling price and a lower purchase price. Conversely, a capital loss arises if the proceeds from the sale of a capital asset are less than the purchase price.
Disposition effect	The disposition effect is an anomaly discovered in behavioral finance. It relates to the tendency of investors to sell shares whose price has increased, while keeping assets that have dropped in value. Description Investors are less willing to recognize losses (which they would be forced to do if they sold assets which had fallen in value), but are more willing to recognize gains.
Ostrich effect	In behavioral finance, the ostrich effect is the avoidance of apparently risky financial situations by pretending they do not exist. The name comes from the common (but false) legend that ostriches bury their heads in the sand to avoid danger. Galai and Sade (2006) explain differences in returns in the fixed income market by using a psychological explanation, which they name the 'ostrich effect,' attributing this anomalous behavior to an aversion to receiving information on potential interim losses.
Cognitive dissonance	Cognitive dissonance is an uncomfortable feeling caused by holding conflicting ideas simultaneously. The theory of cognitive dissonance proposes that people have a motivational drive to reduce dissonance. They do this by changing their attitudes, beliefs, and actions.

Visit Cram101.com for full Practice Exams

12. Behavioral Finance and Technical Analysis

CHAPTER HIGHLIGHTS & NOTES: KEY TERMS, PEOPLE, PLACES, CONCEPTS

Adaptive market hypothesis	The adaptive market hypothesis, as proposed by Andrew Lo, is an attempt to reconcile economic theories based on the efficient market hypothesis (which implies that markets are efficient) with behavioral economics, by applying the principles of evolution to financial interactions: competition, adaptation and natural selection. Under this approach, the traditional models of modern financial economics can coexist with behavioral models. Lo argues that much of what behaviorists cite as counterexamples to economic rationality-loss aversion, overconfidence, overreaction, and other behavioral biases-are, in fact, consistent with an evolutionary model of individuals adapting to a changing environment using simple heuristics.
Book value	In accounting, book value is the value of an asset according to its balance sheet account balance. For assets, the value is based on the original cost of the asset less any depreciation, amortization or Impairment costs made against the asset. Traditionally, a company's book value is its total assets minus intangible assets and liabilities.
Contrarian	In finance, a contrarian is one who attempts to profit by investing in a manner that differs from the conventional wisdom, when the consensus opinion appears to be wrong. A contrarian believes that certain crowd behavior among investors can lead to exploitable mispricings in securities markets. For example, widespread pessimism about a stock can drive a price so low that it overstates the company's risks, and understates its prospects for returning to profitability.
Stock valuation	In financial markets, stock valuation is the method of calculating theoretical values of companies and their stocks. The main use of these methods is to predict future market prices, or more generally, potential market prices, and thus to profit from price movement - stocks that are judged undervalued (with respect to their theoretical value) are bought, while stocks that are judged overvalued are sold, in the expectation that undervalued stocks will, on the whole, rise in value, while overvalued stocks will, on the whole, fall. In the view of fundamental analysis, stock valuation based on fundamentals aims to give an estimate of their intrinsic value of the stock, based on predictions of the future cash flows and profitability of the business.
Dow theory	The Dow theory on stock price movement is a form of technical analysis that includes some aspects of sector rotation. The theory was derived from 255 Wall Street Journal editorials written by Charles H. Dow (1851-1902), journalist, founder and first editor of the Wall Street Journal and co-founder of Dow Jones and Company. Following Dow's death, William Peter Hamilton, Robert Rhea and E. George Schaefer organized and collectively represented Dow theory, based on Dow's editorials.

12. Behavioral Finance and Technical Analysis

CHAPTER HIGHLIGHTS & NOTES: KEY TERMS, PEOPLE, PLACES, CONCEPTS

Bar chart	A bar chart is a chart with rectangular bars with lengths proportional to the values that they represent. The bars can be plotted vertically or horizontally. A vertical bar chart is sometimes called a column bar chart.
Moving average	In statistics, a moving average, rolling mean or running average, is a type of finite impulse response filter used to analyze a set of data points by creating a series of averages of different subsets of the full data set. Given a series of numbers and a fixed subset size, the first element of the moving average is obtained by taking the average of the initial fixed subset of the number series. Then the subset is modified by 'shifting forward', that is excluding the first number of the series and including the next number following the original subset in the series.
Oscillator	An oscillator is a technical analysis indicator that varies over time within a band (above and below a center line, or between set levels). Oscillators are used to discover short-term overbought or oversold conditions. Common oscillators are MACD, ROC, RSI, CCI.
Technical analysis	In finance, technical analysis is a security analysis discipline used for forecasting the direction of prices through the study of past market data, primarily price and volume. Behavioral economics and quantitative analysis use many of the same tools of technical analysis, which, being an aspect of active management, stands in contradiction to much of modern portfolio theory. The efficacy of both technical and fundamental analysis is disputed by the efficient-market hypothesis which states that stock market prices are essentially unpredictable.
Diversification	Diversification is a form of corporate strategy for a company. It seeks to increase profitability through greater sales volume obtained from new products and new markets. Diversification can occur either at the business unit level or at the corporate level.

Visit Cram101.com for full Practice Exams

12. Behavioral Finance and Technical Analysis

CHAPTER QUIZ: KEY TERMS, PEOPLE, PLACES, CONCEPTS

1. The _____ is an anomaly discovered in behavioral finance. It relates to the tendency of investors to sell shares whose price has increased, while keeping assets that have dropped in value. Description

    Investors are less willing to recognize losses (which they would be forced to do if they sold assets which had fallen in value), but are more willing to recognize gains.

    a. Forward exchange
    b. Disposition effect
    c. granularity
    d. Constant elasticity of variance model

2. In financial markets, _____ is the method of calculating theoretical values of companies and their stocks. The main use of these methods is to predict future market prices, or more generally, potential market prices, and thus to profit from price movement - stocks that are judged undervalued (with respect to their theoretical value) are bought, while stocks that are judged overvalued are sold, in the expectation that undervalued stocks will, on the whole, rise in value, while overvalued stocks will, on the whole, fall.

    In the view of fundamental analysis, _____ based on fundamentals aims to give an estimate of their intrinsic value of the stock, based on predictions of the future cash flows and profitability of the business.

    a. Continuing value
    b. granularity
    c. Stock valuation
    d. Build-operate-transfer

3. Behavioral economics and the related field, _____, study the effects of social, cognitive, and emotional factors on the economic decisions of individuals and institutions and the consequences for market prices, returns, and the resource allocation. The fields are primarily concerned with the bounds of rationality of economic agents. Behavioral models typically integrate insights from psychology with neo-classical economic theory.

    a. Virtuous circle
    b. Self-fulfilling prophecy
    c. granularity
    d. Behavioral Finance

4. . In finance, a _____ is one who attempts to profit by investing in a manner that differs from the conventional wisdom, when the consensus opinion appears to be wrong.

    A _____ believes that certain crowd behavior among investors can lead to exploitable mispricings in securities markets. For example, widespread pessimism about a stock can drive a price so low that it overstates the company's risks, and understates its prospects for returning to profitability.

    a. Share repurchase

Visit Cram101.com for full Practice Exams

12. Behavioral Finance and Technical Analysis

CHAPTER QUIZ: KEY TERMS, PEOPLE, PLACES, CONCEPTS

    b. Contrarian
    c. Finance
    d. Build-operate-transfer

5. In accounting, _____ is the value of an asset according to its balance sheet account balance. For assets, the value is based on the original cost of the asset less any depreciation, amortization or Impairment costs made against the asset. Traditionally, a company's _____ is its total assets minus intangible assets and liabilities.

    a. Commuted cash value
    b. Controlling interest
    c. Book value
    d. Deferred financing cost

Visit Cram101.com for full Practice Exams

ANSWER KEY
12. Behavioral Finance and Technical Analysis

1. b
2. c
3. d
4. b
5. c

You can take the complete Chapter Practice Test

for 12. Behavioral Finance and Technical Analysis
on all key terms, persons, places, and concepts.

Online 99 Cents

http://www.epub2174.13.22362.12.cram101.com/

Use www.Cram101.com for all your study needs

including Cram101's online interactive problem solving labs in

chemistry, statistics, mathematics, and more.

13. The Bond Market

CHAPTER OUTLINE: KEY TERMS, PEOPLE, PLACES, CONCEPTS

	Coupon rate
	Current yield
	Maturity date
	Principal
	Yield curve
	Term structure
	Yield to maturity
	Monetary policy
	Mortgage loan
	Bearer bond
	Book entry
	Money supply
	Credit rating
	Bond credit rating
	High-yield bond
	Accrued interest
	Commercial bank
	Margin
	Equipment trust certificate
	Mortgage bond
	Debenture

Visit Cram101.com for full Practice Exams

13. The Bond Market
CHAPTER OUTLINE: KEY TERMS, PEOPLE, PLACES, CONCEPTS

	Collateral
	Securitization
	Duration
	Revenue bond
	Eurobond
	Extendible bond
	Basis point
	Original issue discount
	Valuation
	Capital gain
	Balloon payment
	Serial bond
	Sinking fund
	Refunding

Visit Cram101.com for full Practice Exams

13. The Bond Market

CHAPTER HIGHLIGHTS & NOTES: KEY TERMS, PEOPLE, PLACES, CONCEPTS

Coupon rate	A coupon payment on a bond is a periodic interest payment that the bondholder receives during the time between when the bond is issued and when it matures. Coupons are normally described in terms of the coupon rate, which is calculated by adding the total amount of coupons paid per year and dividing by the bond's face value. For example, if a bond has a face value of $1,000 and a coupon rate of 5%, then it pays total coupons of $50 per year.
Current yield	The current yield, interest yield, income yield, flat yield or running yield is a financial term used in reference to bonds and other fixed-interest securities such as gilts. It is the ratio of the annual interest payment and the bond's current clean price: $$\text{Current yield} = \frac{\text{Annual interest payment}}{\text{Clean price}}.$$ The current yield only therefore refers to the yield of the bond at the current moment. It does not reflect the total return over the life of the bond.
Maturity date	In finance, maturity or maturity date refers to the final payment date of a loan or other financial instrument, at which point the principal (and all remaining interest) is due to be paid. The term fixed maturity is applicable to any form of financial instrument under which the loan is due to be repaid on a fixed date. This includes fixed interest and variable rate loans or debt instruments, whatever they are called, and also other forms of security such as redeemable preference shares, provided their terms of issue specify a date.
Principal	In commercial law, a principal is a person, legal or natural, who authorizes an agent to act to create one or more legal relationships with a third party. This branch of law is called agency and relies on the common law proposition qui facit per alium, facit per se . It is a parallel concept to vicarious liability and strict liability (in which one person is held liable for the acts or omissions of another) in criminal law or torts.
Yield curve	In finance, the yield curve is a curve showing several yields or interest rates across different contract lengths (2 month, 2 year, 20 year, etc.).. for a similar debt contract. The curve shows the relation between the (level of) interest rate and the time to maturity, known as the 'term', of the debt for a given borrower in a given currency.
Term structure	In finance, the yield curve is a curve showing several yields or interest rates across different contract lengths for a similar debt contract. The curve shows the relation between the (level of) interest rate (or cost of borrowing) and the time to maturity, known as the 'term', of the debt for a given borrower in a given currency. For example, the U.S. dollar interest rates paid on U.S.

13. The Bond Market

CHAPTER HIGHLIGHTS & NOTES: KEY TERMS, PEOPLE, PLACES, CONCEPTS

Yield to maturity	The Yield to maturity or redemption yield of a bond or other fixed-interest security, such as gilts, is the internal rate of return (IRR, overall interest rate) earned by an investor who buys the bond today at the market price, assuming that the bond will be held until maturity, and that all coupon and principal payments will be made on schedule. Contrary to popular belief, including concepts often cited in advanced financial literature, Yield to maturity does NOT depend upon a reinvestment of coupon payments. Yield to maturity, rather, is simply the discount rate at which the sum of all future cash flows from the bond (coupons and principal) is equal to the price of the bond.
Monetary policy	Monetary policy is the process by which the monetary authority of a country control the supply of money, often targeting a rate of interest for the purpose of promoting economic growth and stability. The official goals usually include relatively stable prices and low unemployment. Monetary theory provides insight into how to craft optimal monetary policy.
Mortgage loan	A mortgage loan is a loan secured by real property through the use of a mortgage note which evidences the existence of the loan and the encumbrance of that realty through the granting of a mortgage which secures the loan. However, the word mortgage alone, in everyday usage, is most often used to mean mortgage loan. The word mortgage is a French Law term meaning 'death contract', meaning that the pledge ends (dies) when either the obligation is fulfilled or the property is taken through foreclosure.
Bearer bond	A bearer bond is a debt security issued by a business entity, such as a corporation, or by a government. It differs from the more common types of investment securities in that it is unregistered - no records are kept of the owner, or the transactions involving ownership. Whoever physically holds the paper on which the bond is issued owns the instrument.
Book entry	Book entry is a system of tracking ownership of securities where no certificate is given to investors. In the case of book-entry-only (BEO) issues, while investors do not receive certificates, a custodian holds one or more global certificates. Dematerialized securities, in contrast are ones in which no certificates exist, instead, the security issuer or its agent keeps records, usually electronically, of who holds outstanding securities.
Money supply	In economics, the money supply, is the total amount of monetary assets available in an economy at a specific time. There are several ways to define 'money,' but standard measures usually include currency in circulation and demand deposits (depositors' easily accessed assets on the books of financial institutions). Money supply data are recorded and published, usually by the government or the central bank of the country.
Credit rating	A credit rating evaluates the credit worthiness of a debtor, especially a business (company) or a government.

Visit Cram101.com for full Practice Exams

13. The Bond Market

CHAPTER HIGHLIGHTS & NOTES: KEY TERMS, PEOPLE, PLACES, CONCEPTS

	It is an evaluation made by a credit rating agency of the debtor's ability to pay back the debt and the likelihood of default.
	Credit ratings are determined by credit ratings agencies.
Bond credit rating	In investment, the bond credit rating assesses the credit worthiness of a corporation's or government debt issues. It is analogous to credit ratings for individuals.
	The credit rating is a financial indicator to potential investors of debt securities such as bonds. These are assigned by credit rating agencies such as Moody's, Standard & Poor's, and Fitch Ratings to have letter designations (such as AAA, B, CC) which represent the quality of a bond. Bond ratings below BBB-/Baa are considered to be not investment grade and are colloquially called junk bonds.
High-yield bond	In finance, a high-yield bond is a bond that is rated below investment grade. These bonds have a higher risk of default or other adverse credit events, but typically pay higher yields than better quality bonds in order to make them attractive to investors.
	Global issue of high-yield bonds more than doubled in 2003 to nearly $146 billion in securities issued from less than $63 billion in 2002, although this is still less than the record of $150 billion in 1998. Issue is disproportionately centered in the United States, although issuers in Europe, Asia and South Africa have recently turned to high-yield debt in connection with refinancings and acquisitions.
Accrued interest	In finance, accrued Interest is the interest that has accumulated since the principal investment, or since the previous interest payment if there has been one already. For a financial instrument such as a bond, interest is calculated and paid in set intervals. Accrued income is an income which has been accumulated or accrued irrespective to actual receipt, which means event occurred but cash not yet received.
Commercial bank	A commercial bank is a type of financial institution and intermediary. It is a bank that provides transactional, savings, and money market accounts and that accepts time deposits.
	After the implementation of the Glass-Steagall Act, the U.S. Congress required that banks engage only in banking activities, whereas investment banks were limited to capital market activities.
Margin	In finance, a margin is collateral that the holder of a financial instrument has to deposit to cover some or all of the credit risk of their counterparty (most often their broker or an exchange). This risk can arise if the holder has done any of the following:•borrowed cash from the counterparty to buy financial instruments,•sold financial instruments short, or•entered into a derivative contract.
	The collateral can be in the form of cash or securities, and it is deposited in a margin account.

Visit Cram101.com for full Practice Exams

13. The Bond Market

CHAPTER HIGHLIGHTS & NOTES: KEY TERMS, PEOPLE, PLACES, CONCEPTS

Equipment trust certificate	An equipment trust certificate is a financial security used in aircraft finance, most commonly to take advantage of tax benefits in North America. In a typical Equipment trust certificate transaction, a 'trust certificate' is sold to investors in order to finance the purchase of an aircraft by a trust managed on the investors' behalf. The trust then leases the aircraft to an airline, and the trustee routes payments through the trust to the investors. Upon maturity of the note, the airline receives title to the aircraft.
Mortgage bond	A mortgage bond is a bond backed by a pool of mortgages on a real estate asset such as a house. More generally, bonds which are secured by the pledge of specific assets are called mortgage bonds. Mortgage bonds can pay interest in either monthly, quarterly or semiannual periods.
Debenture	In sport, a debenture is defined as a certificate of agreement of loans which is given under the company's stamp and carries an undertaking that the debenture holder will get a fixed return (fixed on the basis of interest rates) and the principal amount whenever the debenture matures. The terms may also include ancillary benefits such as an option to buy tickets at a favourable price, as well as or instead of interest. A large number of sporting organisations have issued debentures to raise money, to allow their fans to gain a financial stake in the club, and to foster a sense of community.
Collateral	In lending agreements, collateral is a borrower's pledge of specific property to a lender, to secure repayment of a loan. The collateral serves as protection for a lender against a borrower's default - that is, any borrower failing to pay the principal and interest under the terms of a loan obligation. If a borrower does default on a loan (due to insolvency or other event), that borrower forfeits (gives up) the property pledged as collateral - and the lender then becomes the owner of the collateral.
Securitization	Securitization is the financial practice of pooling various types of contractual debt such as residential mortgages, commercial mortgages, auto loans or credit card debt obligations and selling said consolidated debt as bonds, pass-through securities, or Collateralized mortgage obligation (CMOs), to various investors. The principal and interest on the debt, underlying the security, is paid back to the various investors regularly. Securities backed by mortgage receivables are called mortgage-backed securities (MBS), while those backed by other types of receivables are asset-backed securities (ABS).
Duration	Duration of a project's terminal element is the number of calendar periods it takes from the time the execution of element starts to the moment it is completed. Do not confuse duration with work. E.g. it takes three days for a snail-mail letter to arrive from point A to point B, whereas the work put into mailing it may be 0.5 hours.

13. The Bond Market

CHAPTER HIGHLIGHTS & NOTES: KEY TERMS, PEOPLE, PLACES, CONCEPTS

Strictly speaking, the phrase Duration of terminal element X is 5 days is incomplete. It fails to specify the following:•the probability with which the completion is expected in the time allotted (since any estimate is only a prediction about the uncertain future, see critical chain)•the resources to be used (sometimes using more resources or different resources speeds things up)•the assumptions which were made•the author of the estimation•the date the estimate was made•the work schedule of the resources•etc.

Revenue bond

A revenue bond is a special type of municipal bond distinguished by its guarantee of repayment solely from revenues generated by a specified revenue-generating entity associated with the purpose of the bonds, rather than from a tax. Unlike general obligation bonds, only the revenues specified in the legal contract between the bond holder and bond issuer are required to be used for repayment of the principal and interest of the bonds; other revenues (notably tax revenues) and the general credit of the issuing agency are not so encumbered. Because the pledge of security is not as great as that of general obligation bonds, revenue bonds may carry a slightly higher interest rate than G.O. bonds; however, they are usually considered the second-most secure type of municipal bonds.

Eurobond

A Eurobond is an international bond that is denominated in a currency not native to the country where it is issued. Also called external bond; 'external bonds which, strictly, are neither Eurobonds nor foreign bonds would also include: foreign currency denominated domestic bonds.

Extendible bond

Extendible bond is a complex bond with the embedded option for a holder to extend its maturity date by a number of years. Such a bond may be considered as a portfolio of a straight, shorter-term bond and a call option to buy a longer-term bond. This relatively rare type of bond works to the advantage of investors during periods of declining interest rates.

Basis point

A basis point is a unit equal to one hundredth of a percentage point, or one part per ten thousand, 1/10000. The same unit is also (rarely) called a permyriad, literally meaning 'for (every) myriad (ten thousand)', and in that context is written with U+2031 ? per ten thousand sign (HTML:) which looks like a percent sign (%) with two extra zeroes at the end (like a stylized form of the four zeros in the denominator, although it originates as a natural extension of the percent (%) and permille (‰) signs).

A basis point is defined as:1 basis point = 1 permyriad = one one-hundredth percent1 bp = 1? = 0.01% = 0.1‰ = 10^{-4} = $1/10000$ = 0.00011% = 100 bp = 100?

It is frequently, but not exclusively, used to express differences in interest rates of less than 1% per year. For example, a difference of 0.10% is equivalent to a change of 10 basis points (e.g. a 4.67% rate increases by 10 basis points to 4.77%).

13. The Bond Market

CHAPTER HIGHLIGHTS & NOTES: KEY TERMS, PEOPLE, PLACES, CONCEPTS

Original issue discount	Original Issue Discount is a type of interest that is not payable as it accrues. Original issue discount is normally created when a debt, usually a bond, is issued at a discount. In effect, selling a bond at a discount converts stated principal into a return on investment, or interest.
Valuation	In finance, valuation is the process of estimating what something is worth. Items that are usually valued are a financial asset or liability. Valuations can be done on assets (for example, investments in marketable securities such as stocks, options, business enterprises, or intangible assets such as patents and trademarks) or on liabilities (e.g., bonds issued by a company).
Capital gain	A capital gain is a profit that results from a disposition of a capital asset, such as stock, bond or real estate, where the amount realized on the disposition exceeds the purchase price. The gain is the difference between a higher selling price and a lower purchase price. Conversely, a capital loss arises if the proceeds from the sale of a capital asset are less than the purchase price.
Balloon payment	A balloon payment is an unusually large payment due at the end of a mortgage or loan. Since the payments are not spread out, this large sum is the final repayment to the lender. Holding back most of a debt and paying it only towards the end of the agreement makes both those last payments and the total amount repaid much larger.
Serial bond	Serial bonds are financial bonds that mature in installments over a period of time. In effect, a $100,000, 5-year serial bond would mature in a $20,000 annuity over a 5-year interval. Bond issues consisting of a series of blocks of securities maturing in sequence, the coupon rate can be different.
Sinking fund	A sinking fund is a fund established by a government agency or business for the purpose of reducing debt by repaying or purchasing outstanding loans and securities held against the entity. It helps keep the borrower liquid so it can repay the bondholder. Historical context

The sinking fund was first used in Great Britain in the 18th century to reduce national debt. |
| Refunding | Refunding occurs when an entity that has issued callable bonds calls those debt securities from the debt holders with the express purpose of reissuing new debt at a lower coupon rate. In essence, the issue of new, lower-interest debt allows the company to prematurely refund the older, higher-interest debt.

On the contrary, NonRefundable Bonds may be callable but they cannot be re-issued with a lower coupon rate. |

Visit Cram101.com for full Practice Exams

13. The Bond Market

CHAPTER QUIZ: KEY TERMS, PEOPLE, PLACES, CONCEPTS

1. In finance, maturity or _____ refers to the final payment date of a loan or other financial instrument, at which point the principal (and all remaining interest) is due to be paid.

   The term fixed maturity is applicable to any form of financial instrument under which the loan is due to be repaid on a fixed date. This includes fixed interest and variable rate loans or debt instruments, whatever they are called, and also other forms of security such as redeemable preference shares, provided their terms of issue specify a date.

   a. granularity
   b. Deviation risk measure
   c. Maturity date
   d. Dynamic risk measure

2. A _____ is a type of financial institution and intermediary. It is a bank that provides transactional, savings, and money market accounts and that accepts time deposits.

   After the implementation of the Glass-Steagall Act, the U.S. Congress required that banks engage only in banking activities, whereas investment banks were limited to capital market activities.

   a. Community development bank
   b. Commercial bank
   c. Interest bearing
   d. Interest-only loan

3. In finance, the yield curve is a curve showing several yields or interest rates across different contract lengths for a similar debt contract. The curve shows the relation between the (level of) interest rate (or cost of borrowing) and the time to maturity, known as the 'term', of the debt for a given borrower in a given currency. For example, the U.S. dollar interest rates paid on U.S. Treasury securities for various maturities are closely watched by many traders, and are commonly plotted on a graph such as the one on the right which is informally called 'the yield curve.' More formal mathematical descriptions of this relation are often called the _____ of interest rates.

   a. Term structure
   b. Jimmy Carter
   c. Stiglitz
   d. Relational contract

4. A coupon payment on a bond is a periodic interest payment that the bondholder receives during the time between when the bond is issued and when it matures.

   Coupons are normally described in terms of the _____, which is calculated by adding the total amount of coupons paid per year and dividing by the bond's face value. For example, if a bond has a face value of $1,000 and a _____ of 5%, then it pays total coupons of $50 per year.

   a. granularity

Visit Cram101.com for full Practice Exams

13. The Bond Market

CHAPTER QUIZ: KEY TERMS, PEOPLE, PLACES, CONCEPTS

    b. Jimmy Carter
    c. Stiglitz
    d. Coupon rate

5. In commercial law, a _____ is a person, legal or natural, who authorizes an agent to act to create one or more legal relationships with a third party. This branch of law is called agency and relies on the common law proposition qui facit per alium, facit per se .

   It is a parallel concept to vicarious liability and strict liability (in which one person is held liable for the acts or omissions of another) in criminal law or torts.

    a. Principal
    b. Refusal to deal
    c. Registered agent
    d. Relational contract

Visit Cram101.com for full Practice Exams

ANSWER KEY
13. The Bond Market

1. c
2. b
3. a
4. d
5. a

You can take the complete Chapter Practice Test

for 13. The Bond Market
on all key terms, persons, places, and concepts.

Online 99 Cents

http://www.epub2174.13.22362.13.cram101.com/

Use www.Cram101.com for all your study needs

including Cram101's online interactive problem solving labs in

chemistry, statistics, mathematics, and more.

14. The Valuation of Fixed-Income Securities

CHAPTER OUTLINE: KEY TERMS, PEOPLE, PLACES, CONCEPTS

- Perpetual bond
- Valuation
- Maturity date
- Capital gain
- Extendible bond
- Preferred stock
- Current yield
- Yield to maturity
- Sinking fund
- Duration
- Convexity
- Commercial bank
- Interest rate swap
- Savings and loan association

Visit Cram101.com for full Practice Exams

14. The Valuation of Fixed-Income Securities

CHAPTER HIGHLIGHTS & NOTES: KEY TERMS, PEOPLE, PLACES, CONCEPTS

Perpetual bond	Perpetual bond, which is also known as a Perpetual or just a Perp, is a bond with no maturity date. Therefore, it may be treated as equity, not as debt. Perpetual bonds pay coupons forever, and the issuer does not have to redeem them.
Valuation	In finance, valuation is the process of estimating what something is worth. Items that are usually valued are a financial asset or liability. Valuations can be done on assets (for example, investments in marketable securities such as stocks, options, business enterprises, or intangible assets such as patents and trademarks) or on liabilities (e.g., bonds issued by a company).
Maturity date	In finance, maturity or maturity date refers to the final payment date of a loan or other financial instrument, at which point the principal (and all remaining interest) is due to be paid. The term fixed maturity is applicable to any form of financial instrument under which the loan is due to be repaid on a fixed date. This includes fixed interest and variable rate loans or debt instruments, whatever they are called, and also other forms of security such as redeemable preference shares, provided their terms of issue specify a date.
Capital gain	A capital gain is a profit that results from a disposition of a capital asset, such as stock, bond or real estate, where the amount realized on the disposition exceeds the purchase price. The gain is the difference between a higher selling price and a lower purchase price. Conversely, a capital loss arises if the proceeds from the sale of a capital asset are less than the purchase price.
Extendible bond	Extendible bond is a complex bond with the embedded option for a holder to extend its maturity date by a number of years. Such a bond may be considered as a portfolio of a straight, shorter-term bond and a call option to buy a longer-term bond. This relatively rare type of bond works to the advantage of investors during periods of declining interest rates.
Preferred stock	Preferred stock is an equity security which may have any combination of features not possessed by common stock including properties of both an equity and a debt instruments, and is generally considered a hybrid instrument. Preferreds are senior (i.e. higher ranking) to common stock, but subordinate to bonds in terms of claim . Preferred stock usually carries no voting rights, but may carry a dividend and may have priority over common stock in the payment of dividends and upon liquidation.
Current yield	The current yield, interest yield, income yield, flat yield or running yield is a financial term used in reference to bonds and other fixed-interest securities such as gilts. It is the ratio of the annual interest payment and the bond's current clean price:

$$\text{Current yield} = \frac{\text{Annual interest payment}}{\text{Clean price}}.$$

14. The Valuation of Fixed-Income Securities

CHAPTER HIGHLIGHTS & NOTES: KEY TERMS, PEOPLE, PLACES, CONCEPTS

	The current yield only therefore refers to the yield of the bond at the current moment. It does not reflect the total return over the life of the bond.
Yield to maturity	The Yield to maturity or redemption yield of a bond or other fixed-interest security, such as gilts, is the internal rate of return (IRR, overall interest rate) earned by an investor who buys the bond today at the market price, assuming that the bond will be held until maturity, and that all coupon and principal payments will be made on schedule. Contrary to popular belief, including concepts often cited in advanced financial literature, Yield to maturity does NOT depend upon a reinvestment of coupon payments. Yield to maturity, rather, is simply the discount rate at which the sum of all future cash flows from the bond (coupons and principal) is equal to the price of the bond.
Sinking fund	A sinking fund is a fund established by a government agency or business for the purpose of reducing debt by repaying or purchasing outstanding loans and securities held against the entity. It helps keep the borrower liquid so it can repay the bondholder. Historical context

The sinking fund was first used in Great Britain in the 18th century to reduce national debt. |
| Duration | Duration of a project's terminal element is the number of calendar periods it takes from the time the execution of element starts to the moment it is completed.

Do not confuse duration with work. E.g. it takes three days for a snail-mail letter to arrive from point A to point B, whereas the work put into mailing it may be 0.5 hours.

Strictly speaking, the phrase Duration of terminal element X is 5 days is incomplete. It fails to specify the following:•the probability with which the completion is expected in the time allotted (since any estimate is only a prediction about the uncertain future, see critical chain)•the resources to be used (sometimes using more resources or different resources speeds things up)•the assumptions which were made•the author of the estimation•the date the estimate was made•the work schedule of the resources•etc. |
| Convexity | In mathematical finance, convexity refers to non-linearities in a financial model. In other words, if the price of an underlying variable changes, the price of an output does not change linearly, but depends on the second derivative (or, loosely speaking, higher-order terms) of the modeling function. Geometrically, the model is no longer flat but curved, and the degree of curvature is called the convexity. |
| Commercial bank | A commercial bank is a type of financial institution and intermediary. It is a bank that provides transactional, savings, and money market accounts and that accepts time deposits. |

14. The Valuation of Fixed-Income Securities

CHAPTER HIGHLIGHTS & NOTES: KEY TERMS, PEOPLE, PLACES, CONCEPTS

	After the implementation of the Glass-Steagall Act, the U.S. Congress required that banks engage only in banking activities, whereas investment banks were limited to capital market activities.
Interest rate swap	An interest rate swap is a popular and highly liquid financial derivative instrument in which two parties agree to exchange interest rate cash flows, based on a specified notional amount from a fixed rate to a floating rate or from one floating rate to another. Interest rate swaps are commonly used for both hedging and speculating. Structure In an interest rate swap, each counterparty agrees to pay either a fixed or floating rate denominated in a particular currency to the other counterparty.
Savings and loan association	A savings and loan association, also known as a thrift, is a financial institution that specializes in accepting savings deposits and making mortgage and other loans. The terms 'S&L' or 'thrift' are mainly used in the United States; similar institutions in the United Kingdom, Ireland and some Commonwealth countries include building societies and trustee savings banks. They are often mutually held (often called mutual savings banks), meaning that the depositors and borrowers are members with voting rights, and have the ability to direct the financial and managerial goals of the organization like the members of a credit union or the policyholders of a mutual insurance company.

CHAPTER QUIZ: KEY TERMS, PEOPLE, PLACES, CONCEPTS

1. The _____ or redemption yield of a bond or other fixed-interest security, such as gilts, is the internal rate of return (IRR, overall interest rate) earned by an investor who buys the bond today at the market price, assuming that the bond will be held until maturity, and that all coupon and principal payments will be made on schedule. Contrary to popular belief, including concepts often cited in advanced financial literature, _____ does NOT depend upon a reinvestment of coupon payments. _____, rather, is simply the discount rate at which the sum of all future cash flows from the bond (coupons and principal) is equal to the price of the bond.

   a. Yield to maturity
   b. Deviation risk measure
   c. Distortion risk measure
   d. Dynamic risk measure

2. In mathematical finance, _____ refers to non-linearities in a financial model. In other words, if the price of an underlying variable changes, the price of an output does not change linearly, but depends on the second derivative (or, loosely speaking, higher-order terms) of the modeling function. Geometrically, the model is no longer flat but curved, and the degree of curvature is called the _____.

14. The Valuation of Fixed-Income Securities

CHAPTER QUIZ: KEY TERMS, PEOPLE, PLACES, CONCEPTS

   a. Correlation swap
   b. Convexity
   c. Current yield
   d. Delta neutral

3. In finance, maturity or _____ refers to the final payment date of a loan or other financial instrument, at which point the principal (and all remaining interest) is due to be paid.

   The term fixed maturity is applicable to any form of financial instrument under which the loan is due to be repaid on a fixed date. This includes fixed interest and variable rate loans or debt instruments, whatever they are called, and also other forms of security such as redeemable preference shares, provided their terms of issue specify a date.

   a. granularity
   b. Virtual bidding
   c. Maturity date
   d. Yellow strip

4. _____, which is also known as a Perpetual or just a Perp, is a bond with no maturity date. Therefore, it may be treated as equity, not as debt. _____s pay coupons forever, and the issuer does not have to redeem them.

   a. Private Activity Bond
   b. Prize Bond
   c. Perpetual bond
   d. RAAM

5. In finance, _____ is the process of estimating what something is worth. Items that are usually valued are a financial asset or liability. _____s can be done on assets (for example, investments in marketable securities such as stocks, options, business enterprises, or intangible assets such as patents and trademarks) or on liabilities (e.g., bonds issued by a company).

   a. Value investing
   b. Valuation
   c. Volatility arbitrage
   d. Yellow strip

Visit Cram101.com for full Practice Exams

ANSWER KEY
14. The Valuation of Fixed-Income Securities

1. a
2. b
3. c
4. c
5. b

You can take the complete Chapter Practice Test

for 14. The Valuation of Fixed-Income Securities
on all key terms, persons, places, and concepts.

Online 99 Cents

http://www.epub2174.13.22362.14.cram101.com/

Use www.Cram101.com for all your study needs

including Cram101's online interactive problem solving labs in

chemistry, statistics, mathematics, and more.

15. Government Securities

CHAPTER OUTLINE: KEY TERMS, PEOPLE, PLACES, CONCEPTS

- Consumer price index
- Commercial bank
- United States Treasury security
- Standard deviation
- Individual retirement accounts
- Inflation-indexed bond
- Government National Mortgage Association
- Mortgage bond
- Mortgage loan
- Collateralized mortgage obligation
- Tranche
- Short sale
- Exchange-traded fund
- General obligation bond
- Revenue bond
- Serial bond
- Sinking fund
- Bond credit rating
- Build America Bonds
- Yield curve

Visit Cram101.com for full Practice Exams

15. Government Securities

CHAPTER HIGHLIGHTS & NOTES: KEY TERMS, PEOPLE, PLACES, CONCEPTS

Consumer price index	A consumer price index measures changes in the price level of consumer goods and services purchased by households. The Consumer price index is defined by the United States Bureau of Labor Statistics as 'a measure of the average change over time in the prices paid by urban consumers for a market basket of consumer goods and services.'
	The Consumer price index is a statistical estimate constructed using the prices of a sample of representative items whose prices are collected periodically. Sub-indexes and sub-sub-indexes are computed for different categories and sub-categories of goods and services, being combined to produce the overall index with weights reflecting their shares in the total of the consumer expenditures covered by the index.
Commercial bank	A commercial bank is a type of financial institution and intermediary. It is a bank that provides transactional, savings, and money market accounts and that accepts time deposits.
	After the implementation of the Glass-Steagall Act, the U.S. Congress required that banks engage only in banking activities, whereas investment banks were limited to capital market activities.
United States Treasury security	A United States Treasury security is a government debt issued by the United States Department of the Treasury through the Bureau of the Public Debt. Treasury securities are the debt financing instruments of the United States federal government, and they are often referred to simply as Treasuries. There are four types of marketable treasury securities: Treasury bills, Treasury notes, Treasury bonds, and Treasury Inflation Protected Securities (TIPS).
Standard deviation	In statistics and probability theory, standard deviation shows how much variation or 'dispersion' exists from the average (mean, or expected value).A low standard deviation indicates that the data points tend to be very close to the mean.High standard deviation indicates that the data points are spread out over a large range of values.
	The standard deviation of a random variable, statistical population, data set, or probability distribution is the square root of its variance. It is algebraically simpler though practically less robust than the average absolute deviation.
Individual retirement accounts	An Individual Retirement Account is a form of 'individual retirement plan', provided by many financial institutions, that provides tax advantages for retirement savings in the United States. An individual retirement account is a type of 'individual retirement arrangement' as described in IRS Publication 590, Individual Retirement Arrangements . The term individual retirement accounts (which is used to describe both individual retirement accounts and the broader category of individual retirement arrangements) encompasses an individual retirement account; a trust or custodial account set up for the exclusive benefit of taxpayers or their beneficiaries; and an individual retirement annuity, by which the taxpayers purchase an annuity contract or an endowment contract from a life insurance company.

15. Government Securities

CHAPTER HIGHLIGHTS & NOTES: KEY TERMS, PEOPLE, PLACES, CONCEPTS

Inflation-indexed bond	Inflation-indexed bonds (also known as inflation-linked bonds or colloquially as linkers) are bonds where the principal is indexed to inflation. They are thus designed to cut out the inflation risk of an investment. The first known inflation-indexed bond was issued by the Massachusetts Bay Company in 1780. The market has grown dramatically since the British government began issuing inflation-linked Gilts in 1981. As of 2008, government-issued inflation-linked bonds comprise over $1.5 trillion of the international debt market.
Government National Mortgage Association	The Government National Mortgage Association or Ginnie Mae, was established in the United States in 1968 to promote home ownership. As a wholly owned government corporation within the Department of Housing and Urban Development (HUD), Ginnie Mae's mission is to expand affordable housing in the U.S. by channeling global capital into the nation's housing finance markets. The Ginnie Mae guarantee allows mortgage lenders to obtain a better price for their loans in the capital markets. Lenders then can use the proceeds to make new mortgage loans available to consumers.
Mortgage bond	A mortgage bond is a bond backed by a pool of mortgages on a real estate asset such as a house. More generally, bonds which are secured by the pledge of specific assets are called mortgage bonds. Mortgage bonds can pay interest in either monthly, quarterly or semiannual periods.
Mortgage loan	A mortgage loan is a loan secured by real property through the use of a mortgage note which evidences the existence of the loan and the encumbrance of that realty through the granting of a mortgage which secures the loan. However, the word mortgage alone, in everyday usage, is most often used to mean mortgage loan. The word mortgage is a French Law term meaning 'death contract', meaning that the pledge ends (dies) when either the obligation is fulfilled or the property is taken through foreclosure.
Collateralized mortgage obligation	A collateralized mortgage obligation is a type of debt security first created in 1983 by the investment banks Salomon Brothers and First Boston for U.S. mortgage lender Freddie Mac. (The Salomon Brothers team was led by Gordon Taylor. The First Boston team was led by Dexter Senft).
Tranche	In structured finance, a tranche is one of a number of related securities offered as part of the same transaction. The word tranche is French for slice, section, series, or portion, and is cognate to English trench ('ditch'). In the financial sense of the word, each bond is a different slice of the deal's risk.
Short sale	A short sale is a sale of real estate in which the sale proceeds fall short of the balance owed on the property's loan. It often occurs when a borrower cannot pay the mortgage loan on their property, but the lender decides that selling the property at a moderate loss is better than pressing the borrower.

15. Government Securities

CHAPTER HIGHLIGHTS & NOTES: KEY TERMS, PEOPLE, PLACES, CONCEPTS

Exchange-traded fund	An exchange-traded fund is an investment fund traded on stock exchanges, much like stocks. An ETF holds assets such as stocks, commodities, or bonds, and trades close to its net asset value over the course of the trading day. Most ETFs track an index, such as the S&P 500 or MSCI EAFE. ETFs may be attractive as investments because of their low costs, tax efficiency, and stock-like features.
General obligation bond	A general obligation bond is a common type of municipal bond in the United States that is secured by a state or local government's pledge to use legally available resources, including tax revenues, to repay bond holders. Most general obligation pledges at the local government level include a pledge to levy a property tax to meet debt service requirements, in which case holders of general obligation bonds have a right to compel the borrowing government to levy that tax to satisfy the local government's obligation. Because property owners are usually reluctant to risk losing their holding due to unpaid property tax bills, credit rating agencies often consider a general obligation pledge to have very strong credit quality and frequently assign them investment grade ratings.
Revenue bond	A revenue bond is a special type of municipal bond distinguished by its guarantee of repayment solely from revenues generated by a specified revenue-generating entity associated with the purpose of the bonds, rather than from a tax. Unlike general obligation bonds, only the revenues specified in the legal contract between the bond holder and bond issuer are required to be used for repayment of the principal and interest of the bonds; other revenues (notably tax revenues) and the general credit of the issuing agency are not so encumbered. Because the pledge of security is not as great as that of general obligation bonds, revenue bonds may carry a slightly higher interest rate than G.O. bonds; however, they are usually considered the second-most secure type of municipal bonds.
Serial bond	Serial bonds are financial bonds that mature in installments over a period of time. In effect, a $100,000, 5-year serial bond would mature in a $20,000 annuity over a 5-year interval. Bond issues consisting of a series of blocks of securities maturing in sequence, the coupon rate can be different.
Sinking fund	A sinking fund is a fund established by a government agency or business for the purpose of reducing debt by repaying or purchasing outstanding loans and securities held against the entity. It helps keep the borrower liquid so it can repay the bondholder. Historical context The sinking fund was first used in Great Britain in the 18th century to reduce national debt.
Bond credit rating	In investment, the bond credit rating assesses the credit worthiness of a corporation's or government debt issues. It is analogous to credit ratings for individuals. The credit rating is a financial indicator to potential investors of debt securities such as bonds.

15. Government Securities

CHAPTER HIGHLIGHTS & NOTES: KEY TERMS, PEOPLE, PLACES, CONCEPTS

	These are assigned by credit rating agencies such as Moody's, Standard & Poor's, and Fitch Ratings to have letter designations (such as AAA, B, CC) which represent the quality of a bond. Bond ratings below BBB-/Baa are considered to be not investment grade and are colloquially called junk bonds.
Build America Bonds	Build America Bonds are taxable municipal bonds that carry special tax credits and federal subsidies for either the bond issuer or the bondholder. Build America Bonds were created under Section 1531 of Title I of Division B of the American Recovery and Reinvestment Act that U.S. President Barack Obama signed into law on February 17, 2009. The program expired December 31, 2010. Purpose of and eligibility for Build America Bonds

The purpose of Build America Bonds is to reduce the cost of borrowing for state and local government issuers and governmental agencies. |
| Yield curve | In finance, the yield curve is a curve showing several yields or interest rates across different contract lengths (2 month, 2 year, 20 year, etc.).. for a similar debt contract. The curve shows the relation between the (level of) interest rate and the time to maturity, known as the 'term', of the debt for a given borrower in a given currency. |

CHAPTER QUIZ: KEY TERMS, PEOPLE, PLACES, CONCEPTS

1. An _____ is an investment fund traded on stock exchanges, much like stocks. An ETF holds assets such as stocks, commodities, or bonds, and trades close to its net asset value over the course of the trading day. Most ETFs track an index, such as the S&P 500 or MSCI EAFE. ETFs may be attractive as investments because of their low costs, tax efficiency, and stock-like features.

    a. Exchange-traded fund
    b. IFund
    c. Income fund
    d. Index fund

2. . A _____ is a type of financial institution and intermediary. It is a bank that provides transactional, savings, and money market accounts and that accepts time deposits.

    After the implementation of the Glass-Steagall Act, the U.S. Congress required that banks engage only in banking activities, whereas investment banks were limited to capital market activities.

    a. Community development bank
    b. backdating

Visit Cram101.com for full Practice Exams

15. Government Securities

CHAPTER QUIZ: KEY TERMS, PEOPLE, PLACES, CONCEPTS

    c. disclosure
    d. Commercial bank

3. A _____ is a government debt issued by the United States Department of the Treasury through the Bureau of the Public Debt. Treasury securities are the debt financing instruments of the United States federal government, and they are often referred to simply as Treasuries. There are four types of marketable treasury securities: Treasury bills, Treasury notes, Treasury bonds, and Treasury Inflation Protected Securities (TIPS).

    a. Electronic Data-Gathering, Analysis, and Retrieval system
    b. University of Strathclyde
    c. American Bar Association
    d. United States Treasury security

4. A _____ measures changes in the price level of consumer goods and services purchased by households. The _____ is defined by the United States Bureau of Labor Statistics as 'a measure of the average change over time in the prices paid by urban consumers for a market basket of consumer goods and services.'

The _____ is a statistical estimate constructed using the prices of a sample of representative items whose prices are collected periodically. Sub-indexes and sub-sub-indexes are computed for different categories and sub-categories of goods and services, being combined to produce the overall index with weights reflecting their shares in the total of the consumer expenditures covered by the index.

    a. Higher Education Price Index
    b. backdating
    c. Consumer price index
    d. Receivable Turnover Ratio

5. In statistics and probability theory, _____ shows how much variation or 'dispersion' exists from the average (mean, or expected value). A low _____ indicates that the data points tend to be very close to the mean. High _____ indicates that the data points are spread out over a large range of values.

The _____ of a random variable, statistical population, data set, or probability distribution is the square root of its variance. It is algebraically simpler though practically less robust than the average absolute deviation.

    a. Standard deviation
    b. Quantile
    c. Quartile
    d. frequency distribution

Visit Cram101.com for full Practice Exams

ANSWER KEY
15. Government Securities

1. a
2. d
3. d
4. c
5. a

You can take the complete Chapter Practice Test

for 15. Government Securities
on all key terms, persons, places, and concepts.

Online 99 Cents

http://www.epub2174.13.22362.15.cram101.com/

Use www.Cram101.com for all your study needs

including Cram101's online interactive problem solving labs in

chemistry, statistics, mathematics, and more.

16. Convertible Bonds and Convertible Preferred Stock

CHAPTER OUTLINE: KEY TERMS, PEOPLE, PLACES, CONCEPTS

	Coupon rate
	Sinking fund
	Valuation
	Convertible security
	Short sale
	Capital gain
	Preferred stock

CHAPTER HIGHLIGHTS & NOTES: KEY TERMS, PEOPLE, PLACES, CONCEPTS

Coupon rate	A coupon payment on a bond is a periodic interest payment that the bondholder receives during the time between when the bond is issued and when it matures. Coupons are normally described in terms of the coupon rate, which is calculated by adding the total amount of coupons paid per year and dividing by the bond's face value. For example, if a bond has a face value of $1,000 and a coupon rate of 5%, then it pays total coupons of $50 per year.
Sinking fund	A sinking fund is a fund established by a government agency or business for the purpose of reducing debt by repaying or purchasing outstanding loans and securities held against the entity. It helps keep the borrower liquid so it can repay the bondholder. Historical context The sinking fund was first used in Great Britain in the 18th century to reduce national debt.
Valuation	In finance, valuation is the process of estimating what something is worth. Items that are usually valued are a financial asset or liability. Valuations can be done on assets (for example, investments in marketable securities such as stocks, options, business enterprises, or intangible assets such as patents and trademarks) or on liabilities (e.g., bonds issued by a company).
Convertible security	A convertible security is a security that can be converted into another security.

Visit Cram101.com for full Practice Exams

16. Convertible Bonds and Convertible Preferred Stock

CHAPTER HIGHLIGHTS & NOTES: KEY TERMS, PEOPLE, PLACES, CONCEPTS

	Convertible securities may be convertible bonds or preferred stocks that pay regular interest and can be converted into shares of common stock (sometimes conditioned on the stock price appreciating to a predetermined level). Warrants are equity convertible securities.
Short sale	A short sale is a sale of real estate in which the sale proceeds fall short of the balance owed on the property's loan. It often occurs when a borrower cannot pay the mortgage loan on their property, but the lender decides that selling the property at a moderate loss is better than pressing the borrower. Both parties consent to the short sale process, because it allows them to avoid foreclosure, which involves hefty fees for the bank and poorer credit report outcomes for the borrowers.
Capital gain	A capital gain is a profit that results from a disposition of a capital asset, such as stock, bond or real estate, where the amount realized on the disposition exceeds the purchase price. The gain is the difference between a higher selling price and a lower purchase price. Conversely, a capital loss arises if the proceeds from the sale of a capital asset are less than the purchase price.
Preferred stock	Preferred stock is an equity security which may have any combination of features not possessed by common stock including properties of both an equity and a debt instruments, and is generally considered a hybrid instrument. Preferreds are senior (i.e. higher ranking) to common stock, but subordinate to bonds in terms of claim .
	Preferred stock usually carries no voting rights, but may carry a dividend and may have priority over common stock in the payment of dividends and upon liquidation.

CHAPTER QUIZ: KEY TERMS, PEOPLE, PLACES, CONCEPTS

1. A _____ is a security that can be converted into another security. _____(ies) may be convertible bonds or preferred stocks that pay regular interest and can be converted into shares of common stock (sometimes conditioned on the stock price appreciating to a predetermined level). Warrants are equity _____(ies).

    a. Direct holding system
    b. Distressed lending
    c. Foreign security
    d. Convertible security

2. . In finance, _____ is the process of estimating what something is worth. Items that are usually valued are a financial asset or liability. _____s can be done on assets (for example, investments in marketable securities such as stocks, options, business enterprises, or intangible assets such as patents and trademarks) or on liabilities (e.g., bonds issued by a company).

16. Convertible Bonds and Convertible Preferred Stock

CHAPTER QUIZ: KEY TERMS, PEOPLE, PLACES, CONCEPTS

   a. Value investing
   b. Virtual bidding
   c. Valuation
   d. Yellow strip

3. A _____ is a sale of real estate in which the sale proceeds fall short of the balance owed on the property's loan. It often occurs when a borrower cannot pay the mortgage loan on their property, but the lender decides that selling the property at a moderate loss is better than pressing the borrower. Both parties consent to the _____ process, because it allows them to avoid foreclosure, which involves hefty fees for the bank and poorer credit report outcomes for the borrowers.

   a. Speculative fever
   b. Distressed lending
   c. Foreign security
   d. Short sale

4. A coupon payment on a bond is a periodic interest payment that the bondholder receives during the time between when the bond is issued and when it matures.

   Coupons are normally described in terms of the _____, which is calculated by adding the total amount of coupons paid per year and dividing by the bond's face value. For example, if a bond has a face value of $1,000 and a _____ of 5%, then it pays total coupons of $50 per year.

   a. granularity
   b. Jimmy Carter
   c. Stiglitz
   d. Coupon rate

5. A _____ is a fund established by a government agency or business for the purpose of reducing debt by repaying or purchasing outstanding loans and securities held against the entity. It helps keep the borrower liquid so it can repay the bondholder. Historical context

   The _____ was first used in Great Britain in the 18th century to reduce national debt.

   a. Small business financing
   b. Smaller reporting company
   c. Special purpose company
   d. Sinking fund

ANSWER KEY
16. Convertible Bonds and Convertible Preferred Stock

1. d
2. c
3. d
4. d
5. d

You can take the complete Chapter Practice Test

for 16. Convertible Bonds and Convertible Preferred Stock
on all key terms, persons, places, and concepts.

Online 99 Cents

http://www.epub2174.13.22362.16.cram101.com/

Use www.Cram101.com for all your study needs

including Cram101's online interactive problem solving labs in

chemistry, statistics, mathematics, and more.

17. An Introduction to Options

CHAPTER OUTLINE: KEY TERMS, PEOPLE, PLACES, CONCEPTS

	Call option
	Put option
	Futures price
	Short sale
	Leverage
	Covered call
	Married put
	Open interest
	Systematic risk
	Stock index

CHAPTER HIGHLIGHTS & NOTES: KEY TERMS, PEOPLE, PLACES, CONCEPTS

Call option — A call option, often simply labeled a 'call', is a financial contract between two parties, the buyer and the seller of this type of option. The buyer of the call option has the right, but not the obligation to buy an agreed quantity of a particular commodity or financial instrument (the underlying) from the seller of the option at a certain time (the expiration date) for a certain price (the strike price). The seller is obligated to sell the commodity or financial instrument should the buyer so decide.

Put option — A put or put option is a contract between two parties to exchange an asset (the underlying), at a specified price (the strike), by a predetermined date (the expiry or maturity). One party, the buyer of the put, has the right, but not an obligation, to re-sell the asset at the strike price by the future date, while the other party, the seller of the put, has the obligation to repurchase the asset at the strike price if the buyer exercises the option.

If the strike is K, and at time t the value of the underlying is $S(t)$, then in an American option the buyer can exercise the put for a payout of $K-S(t)$ up until the option's maturity time T.

Visit Cram101.com for full Practice Exams

17. An Introduction to Options

CHAPTER HIGHLIGHTS & NOTES: KEY TERMS, PEOPLE, PLACES, CONCEPTS

Futures price	In finance, a futures contract (more colloquially, futures) is a standardized contract between two parties to buy or sell a specified asset of standardized quantity and quality for a price agreed upon today (the futures price, the delivery date. The contracts are negotiated at a futures exchange, which acts as an intermediary between the two parties. The party agreeing to buy the underlying asset in the future, the 'buyer' of the contract, is said to be 'long', and the party agreeing to sell the asset in the future, the 'seller' of the contract, is said to be 'short'.
Short sale	A short sale is a sale of real estate in which the sale proceeds fall short of the balance owed on the property's loan. It often occurs when a borrower cannot pay the mortgage loan on their property, but the lender decides that selling the property at a moderate loss is better than pressing the borrower. Both parties consent to the short sale process, because it allows them to avoid foreclosure, which involves hefty fees for the bank and poorer credit report outcomes for the borrowers.
Leverage	In negotiation, leverage is the ability to influence the other side to move closer to one's negotiating position. Types of leverage include positive leverage, negative leverage, and normative leverage. Normative Leverage Normative leverage is the application of general norms or the other party's standards and norms to advance one's own arguments for one's own good.
Covered call	A covered call is a financial market transaction in which the seller of call options owns the corresponding amount of the underlying instrument, such as shares of a stock or other securities. If a trader buys the underlying instrument at the same time the trader sells the call, the strategy is often called a 'buy-write' strategy. In equilibrium, the strategy has the same payoffs as writing a put option.
Married put	A married put, is a portfolio strategy where an investor buys shares of a stock and, at the same time, enough put options to cover those shares. The term 'protective put' highlights the use of this strategy as a hedge, or insurance, on the invested stock. The buyer of a put protects himself from a drop in the stock price below the strike price of the put.
Open interest	Open interest refers to the total number of derivative contracts, like futures and options, that have not been settled in the immediately previous time period for a specific underlying security. A large open interest indicates more activity and liquidity for the contract. For each buyer of a futures contract there must be a seller.

17. An Introduction to Options

CHAPTER HIGHLIGHTS & NOTES: KEY TERMS, PEOPLE, PLACES, CONCEPTS

Systematic risk	In finance and economics, systematic risk is vulnerability to events which affect aggregate outcomes such as broad market returns, total economy-wide resource holdings, or aggregate income. In many contexts, events like earthquakes and major weather catastrophes pose aggregate risks-they affect not only the distribution but also the total amount of resources. If every possible outcome of a stochastic economic process is characterized by the same aggregate result (but potentially different distributional outcomes), then the process has no aggregate risk.
Stock index	A stock index is a method of measuring the value of a section of the stock market. It is computed from the prices of selected stocks (sometimes a weighted average). It is a tool used by investors and financial managers to describe the market, and to compare the return on specific investments.

CHAPTER QUIZ: KEY TERMS, PEOPLE, PLACES, CONCEPTS

1. A _____ is a financial market transaction in which the seller of call options owns the corresponding amount of the underlying instrument, such as shares of a stock or other securities. If a trader buys the underlying instrument at the same time the trader sells the call, the strategy is often called a 'buy-write' strategy. In equilibrium, the strategy has the same payoffs as writing a put option.

    a. Covered call
    b. Credit spread
    c. Foreign-exchange option
    d. Kansas City Board of Trade

2. A _____, often simply labeled a 'call', is a financial contract between two parties, the buyer and the seller of this type of option. The buyer of the _____ has the right, but not the obligation to buy an agreed quantity of a particular commodity or financial instrument (the underlying) from the seller of the option at a certain time (the expiration date) for a certain price (the strike price). The seller is obligated to sell the commodity or financial instrument should the buyer so decide.

    a. Call option
    b. Chooser option
    c. Commodore option
    d. Compound option

3. . In negotiation, _____ is the ability to influence the other side to move closer to one's negotiating position.

    Types of _____ include positive _____, negative _____, and normative _____. Normative _____

Visit Cram101.com for full Practice Exams

17. An Introduction to Options

CHAPTER QUIZ: KEY TERMS, PEOPLE, PLACES, CONCEPTS

Normative _____ is the application of general norms or the other party's standards and norms to advance one's own arguments for one's own good.

- a. Location intelligence
- b. Leverage
- c. Management consulting
- d. Market segmentation index

4. A _____ is a sale of real estate in which the sale proceeds fall short of the balance owed on the property's loan. It often occurs when a borrower cannot pay the mortgage loan on their property, but the lender decides that selling the property at a moderate loss is better than pressing the borrower. Both parties consent to the _____ process, because it allows them to avoid foreclosure, which involves hefty fees for the bank and poorer credit report outcomes for the borrowers.

- a. Speculative fever
- b. Risk reversal
- c. Short sale
- d. Spread option

5. A _____, is a portfolio strategy where an investor buys shares of a stock and, at the same time, enough put options to cover those shares.

The term 'protective put' highlights the use of this strategy as a hedge, or insurance, on the invested stock. The buyer of a put protects himself from a drop in the stock price below the strike price of the put.

- a. Mountain range
- b. Married put
- c. Naked put
- d. Net volatility

ANSWER KEY
17. An Introduction to Options

1. a
2. a
3. b
4. c
5. b

You can take the complete Chapter Practice Test

for 17. An Introduction to Options
on all key terms, persons, places, and concepts.

Online 99 Cents

http://www.epub2174.13.22362.17.cram101.com/

Use www.Cram101.com for all your study needs

including Cram101's online interactive problem solving labs in

chemistry, statistics, mathematics, and more.

18. Option Valuation and Strategies

CHAPTER OUTLINE: KEY TERMS, PEOPLE, PLACES, CONCEPTS

	Valuation
	Employee stock option
	Put-call parity
	Stock index
	Covered call
	Standard deviation
	Bear spread
	Bull spread
	Married put

CHAPTER HIGHLIGHTS & NOTES: KEY TERMS, PEOPLE, PLACES, CONCEPTS

Valuation	In finance, valuation is the process of estimating what something is worth. Items that are usually valued are a financial asset or liability. Valuations can be done on assets (for example, investments in marketable securities such as stocks, options, business enterprises, or intangible assets such as patents and trademarks) or on liabilities (e.g., bonds issued by a company).
Employee stock option	An employee stock option is a call option on the common stock of a company, granted by the company to an employee as part of the employee's remuneration package.
	Stock option expensing became a controversy in the early 2000s, and it was eventually determined by the Financial Accounting Standards Board that the options should be expensed at their fair value as of the grant date. Objectives
	Many companies use employee stock options plans to retain and attract employees, the objective being to give employees an incentive to behave in ways that will boost the company's stock price.

Visit Cram101.com for full Practice Exams

18. Option Valuation and Strategies

CHAPTER HIGHLIGHTS & NOTES: KEY TERMS, PEOPLE, PLACES, CONCEPTS

Put-call parity	In financial mathematics, put-call parity defines a relationship between the price of a European call option and European put option, both with the identical strike price and expiry, namely that a portfolio of long a call option and short a put option is equivalent to (and hence has the same value as) a single forward contract at this strike price and expiry. This is because if the price at expiry is above the strike price, the call will be exercised, while if it is below, the put will be exercised, and thus in either case one unit of the asset will be purchased for the strike price, exactly as in a forward contract. The validity of this relationship requires that certain assumptions be satisfied; these are specified and the relationship derived below.
Stock index	A stock index is a method of measuring the value of a section of the stock market. It is computed from the prices of selected stocks (sometimes a weighted average). It is a tool used by investors and financial managers to describe the market, and to compare the return on specific investments.
Covered call	A covered call is a financial market transaction in which the seller of call options owns the corresponding amount of the underlying instrument, such as shares of a stock or other securities. If a trader buys the underlying instrument at the same time the trader sells the call, the strategy is often called a 'buy-write' strategy. In equilibrium, the strategy has the same payoffs as writing a put option.
Standard deviation	In statistics and probability theory, standard deviation shows how much variation or 'dispersion' exists from the average (mean, or expected value).A low standard deviation indicates that the data points tend to be very close to the mean.High standard deviation indicates that the data points are spread out over a large range of values. The standard deviation of a random variable, statistical population, data set, or probability distribution is the square root of its variance. It is algebraically simpler though practically less robust than the average absolute deviation.
Bear spread	In options trading, a bear spread is a bearish, vertical spread options strategy that can be used when the options trader is moderately bearish on the underlying security. Because of put-call parity, a bear spread can be constructed using either put options or call options. If constructed using calls, it is a bear call spread.
Bull spread	In options trading, a bull spread is a bullish, vertical spread options strategy that is designed to profit from a moderate rise in the price of the underlying security. Because of put-call parity, a bull spread can be constructed using either put options or call options. If constructed using calls, it is a bull call spread.

18. Option Valuation and Strategies

CHAPTER HIGHLIGHTS & NOTES: KEY TERMS, PEOPLE, PLACES, CONCEPTS

Married put	A married put, is a portfolio strategy where an investor buys shares of a stock and, at the same time, enough put options to cover those shares. The term 'protective put' highlights the use of this strategy as a hedge, or insurance, on the invested stock. The buyer of a put protects himself from a drop in the stock price below the strike price of the put.

CHAPTER QUIZ: KEY TERMS, PEOPLE, PLACES, CONCEPTS

1. In options trading, a _____ is a bullish, vertical spread options strategy that is designed to profit from a moderate rise in the price of the underlying security.

   Because of put-call parity, a _____ can be constructed using either put options or call options. If constructed using calls, it is a bull call spread.

   a. Butterfly
   b. Calendar spread
   c. Bull spread
   d. Cash or share option

2. In financial mathematics, _____ defines a relationship between the price of a European call option and European put option, both with the identical strike price and expiry, namely that a portfolio of long a call option and short a put option is equivalent to (and hence has the same value as) a single forward contract at this strike price and expiry. This is because if the price at expiry is above the strike price, the call will be exercised, while if it is below, the put will be exercised, and thus in either case one unit of the asset will be purchased for the strike price, exactly as in a forward contract.

   The validity of this relationship requires that certain assumptions be satisfied; these are specified and the relationship derived below.

   a. Put-call parity
   b. QuantLib
   c. Range accrual
   d. Rational pricing

3. . A _____ is a financial market transaction in which the seller of call options owns the corresponding amount of the underlying instrument, such as shares of a stock or other securities. If a trader buys the underlying instrument at the same time the trader sells the call, the strategy is often called a 'buy-write' strategy. In equilibrium, the strategy has the same payoffs as writing a put option.

Visit Cram101.com for full Practice Exams

18. Option Valuation and Strategies

CHAPTER QUIZ: KEY TERMS, PEOPLE, PLACES, CONCEPTS

   a. Credit default option
   b. Covered call
   c. Foreign-exchange option
   d. Kansas City Board of Trade

4. A _____ is a method of measuring the value of a section of the stock market. It is computed from the prices of selected stocks (sometimes a weighted average). It is a tool used by investors and financial managers to describe the market, and to compare the return on specific investments.

   a. Capitalization-weighted
   b. granularity
   c. Stock index
   d. Rational pricing

5. In finance, _____ is the process of estimating what something is worth. Items that are usually valued are a financial asset or liability. _____s can be done on assets (for example, investments in marketable securities such as stocks, options, business enterprises, or intangible assets such as patents and trademarks) or on liabilities (e.g., bonds issued by a company).

   a. Value investing
   b. Valuation
   c. Volatility arbitrage
   d. Yellow strip

ANSWER KEY
18. Option Valuation and Strategies

1. c
2. a
3. b
4. c
5. b

You can take the complete Chapter Practice Test

for 18. Option Valuation and Strategies
on all key terms, persons, places, and concepts.

Online 99 Cents

http://www.epub2174.13.22362.18.cram101.com/

Use www.Cram101.com for all your study needs

including Cram101's online interactive problem solving labs in

chemistry, statistics, mathematics, and more.

19. Commodity and Financial Futures

CHAPTER OUTLINE: KEY TERMS, PEOPLE, PLACES, CONCEPTS

- Futures contract
- Chicago Board of Trade
- Chicago Mercantile Exchange
- Futures price
- Open interest
- Commodity Futures Trading Commission
- Leverage
- Forward contract
- Exchange-traded note
- Financial future
- Stock index
- Covered call
- Index arbitrage
- Married put
- Triple witching hour
- Currency swap
- Interest rate swap
- Credit default swap

Visit Cram101.com for full Practice Exams

19. Commodity and Financial Futures

CHAPTER HIGHLIGHTS & NOTES: KEY TERMS, PEOPLE, PLACES, CONCEPTS

Futures contract	In finance, a futures contract is a standardized contract between two parties to buy or sell a specified asset of standardized quantity and quality for a price agreed upon today (the futures price or strike price) with delivery and payment occurring at a specified future date, the delivery date. The contracts are negotiated at a futures exchange, which acts as an intermediary between the two parties. The party agreeing to buy the underlying asset in the future, the 'buyer' of the contract, is said to be 'long', and the party agreeing to sell the asset in the future, the 'seller' of the contract, is said to be 'short'.
Chicago Board of Trade	The Chicago Board of Trade established in 1848, is the world's oldest futures and options exchange. More than 50 different options and futures contracts are traded by over 3,600 Chicago Board of Trade members through open outcry and eTrading. Volumes at the exchange in 2003 were a record breaking 454 million contracts.
Chicago Mercantile Exchange	The Chicago Mercantile Exchange (often called 'the Chicago Merc,' or 'the Merc') is an American financial and commodity derivative exchange based in Chicago and located at 20 S. Wacker Drive. The Chicago Mercantile Exchange was founded in 1898 as the Chicago Butter and Egg Board, an agricultural commodities exchange. Originally, the exchange was a non-profit organization.
Futures price	In finance, a futures contract (more colloquially, futures) is a standardized contract between two parties to buy or sell a specified asset of standardized quantity and quality for a price agreed upon today (the futures price, the delivery date. The contracts are negotiated at a futures exchange, which acts as an intermediary between the two parties. The party agreeing to buy the underlying asset in the future, the 'buyer' of the contract, is said to be 'long', and the party agreeing to sell the asset in the future, the 'seller' of the contract, is said to be 'short'.
Open interest	Open interest refers to the total number of derivative contracts, like futures and options, that have not been settled in the immediately previous time period for a specific underlying security. A large open interest indicates more activity and liquidity for the contract. For each buyer of a futures contract there must be a seller.
Commodity Futures Trading Commission	The U.S. Commodity Futures Trading Commission is an independent agency of the United States government that regulates futures and option markets. The Commodity Futures Trading Commission Act of 1974 (P.L. 93-463) created the Commodity Futures Trading Commission, to replace the U.S. Department of Agriculture's Commodity Exchange Authority, as the independent federal agency responsible for regulating the futures trading industry. The Act made extensive changes in the basic authority of Commodity Exchange Act of 1936, which itself had made extensive changes in the original Grain Futures Act of 1923. (7 U.S.C. 1 et seq)..
Leverage	In negotiation, leverage is the ability to influence the other side to move closer to one's negotiating position.

19. Commodity and Financial Futures

CHAPTER HIGHLIGHTS & NOTES: KEY TERMS, PEOPLE, PLACES, CONCEPTS

	Types of leverage include positive leverage, negative leverage, and normative leverage. Normative Leverage
	Normative leverage is the application of general norms or the other party's standards and norms to advance one's own arguments for one's own good.
Forward contract	In finance, a forward contract is a non-standardized contract between two parties to buy or sell an asset at a specified future time at a price agreed upon today. This is in contrast to a spot contract, which is an agreement to buy or sell an asset today. The party agreeing to buy the underlying asset in the future assumes a long position, and the party agreeing to sell the asset in the future assumes a short position.
Exchange-traded note	An exchange-traded note is a senior, unsecured, unsubordinated debt security issued by an underwriting bank. Similar to other debt securities, Exchange traded notes have a maturity date and are backed only by the credit of the issuer.
	Exchange traded notes are designed to provide investors access to the returns of various market benchmarks.
Financial future	A financial future is a futures contract on a short term interest rate (STIR). Contracts vary, but are often defined on an interest rate index such as 3-month sterling or US dollar LIBOR.
	They are traded across a wide range of currencies, including the G12 country currencies and many others.
Stock index	A stock index is a method of measuring the value of a section of the stock market. It is computed from the prices of selected stocks (sometimes a weighted average). It is a tool used by investors and financial managers to describe the market, and to compare the return on specific investments.
Covered call	A covered call is a financial market transaction in which the seller of call options owns the corresponding amount of the underlying instrument, such as shares of a stock or other securities. If a trader buys the underlying instrument at the same time the trader sells the call, the strategy is often called a 'buy-write' strategy. In equilibrium, the strategy has the same payoffs as writing a put option.
Index arbitrage	Index arbitrage is a subset of statistical arbitrage focusing on index components.
	The idea is that an index (such as S&P 500 or Russell 2000) is made up of several components (in the example, 500 large US stocks picked by S&P to represent the US market) that influence the index price in a different manner.

Visit Cram101.com for full Practice Exams

19. Commodity and Financial Futures

CHAPTER HIGHLIGHTS & NOTES: KEY TERMS, PEOPLE, PLACES, CONCEPTS

Married put	A married put, is a portfolio strategy where an investor buys shares of a stock and, at the same time, enough put options to cover those shares. The term 'protective put' highlights the use of this strategy as a hedge, or insurance, on the invested stock. The buyer of a put protects himself from a drop in the stock price below the strike price of the put.
Triple witching hour	Triple witching hour is the last hour of the stock market trading session (3:00-4:00 P.M., New York Time) on the third Friday of every March, June, September, and December. Those days are the expiration of three kinds of securities:•Stock market index futures;•Stock market index options;•Stock options The simultaneous expirations generally increases the trading volume of options, futures and the underlying stocks, and occasionally increases volatility of prices of related securities. On those same days in March, June, September, and December, Single-stock futures also expire, so that the final hour on those days is sometimes referred to as the quadruple witching hour.
Currency swap	A currency swap is a foreign-exchange agreement between two institute to exchange aspects (namely the principal and/or interest payments) of a loan in one currency for equivalent aspects of an equal in net present value loan in another currency. Currency swaps are motivated by comparative advantage. A currency swap should be distinguished from a central bank liquidity swap.
Interest rate swap	An interest rate swap is a popular and highly liquid financial derivative instrument in which two parties agree to exchange interest rate cash flows, based on a specified notional amount from a fixed rate to a floating rate or from one floating rate to another. Interest rate swaps are commonly used for both hedging and speculating. Structure In an interest rate swap, each counterparty agrees to pay either a fixed or floating rate denominated in a particular currency to the other counterparty.
Credit default swap	A credit default swap is a financial swap agreement that the seller of the CDS will compensate the buyer in the event of a loan default or other credit event. The buyer of the CDS makes a series of payments (the CDS 'fee' or 'spread') to the seller and, in exchange, receives a payoff if the loan defaults. In the event of default the buyer of the CDS receives compensation (usually the face value of the loan), and the seller of the CDS takes possession of the defaulted loan.

19. Commodity and Financial Futures

CHAPTER QUIZ: KEY TERMS, PEOPLE, PLACES, CONCEPTS

1. _____ is the last hour of the stock market trading session (3:00-4:00 P.M., New York Time) on the third Friday of every March, June, September, and December. Those days are the expiration of three kinds of securities:•Stock market index futures;•Stock market index options;•Stock options

   The simultaneous expirations generally increases the trading volume of options, futures and the underlying stocks, and occasionally increases volatility of prices of related securities.

   On those same days in March, June, September, and December, Single-stock futures also expire, so that the final hour on those days is sometimes referred to as the quadruple witching hour.

   a. Volatility clustering
   b. Volatility swap
   c. Triple witching hour
   d. Currency option

2. In finance, a _____ is a standardized contract between two parties to buy or sell a specified asset of standardized quantity and quality for a price agreed upon today (the futures price or strike price) with delivery and payment occurring at a specified future date, the delivery date. The contracts are negotiated at a futures exchange, which acts as an intermediary between the two parties. The party agreeing to buy the underlying asset in the future, the 'buyer' of the contract, is said to be 'long', and the party agreeing to sell the asset in the future, the 'seller' of the contract, is said to be 'short'.

   a. Loan credit default swap index
   b. Futures contract
   c. Mercado Abierto Electrnico
   d. Mexican Derivatives Exchange

3. _____ is a subset of statistical arbitrage focusing on index components.

   The idea is that an index (such as S&P 500 or Russell 2000) is made up of several components (in the example, 500 large US stocks picked by S&P to represent the US market) that influence the index price in a different manner.

   For instance, there are leaders (components that react first to market impact) and laggers (the opposite).

   a. Indifference price
   b. Interest rate
   c. Index arbitrage
   d. ExMark

4. . The _____ established in 1848, is the world's oldest futures and options exchange. More than 50 different options and futures contracts are traded by over 3,600 _____ members through open outcry and eTrading. Volumes at the exchange in 2003 were a record breaking 454 million contracts.

   a. granularity

Visit Cram101.com for full Practice Exams

19. Commodity and Financial Futures

CHAPTER QUIZ: KEY TERMS, PEOPLE, PLACES, CONCEPTS

    b. Local volatility
    c. Mercado Abierto Electrnico
    d. Chicago Board of Trade

5. _____ refers to the total number of derivative contracts, like futures and options, that have not been settled in the immediately previous time period for a specific underlying security. A large _____ indicates more activity and liquidity for the contract.

For each buyer of a futures contract there must be a seller.

    a. Interest rate derivative
    b. U.S. Futures Exchange
    c. Underlying
    d. Open interest

Visit Cram101.com for full Practice Exams

ANSWER KEY
19. Commodity and Financial Futures

1. c
2. b
3. c
4. d
5. d

You can take the complete Chapter Practice Test

for 19. Commodity and Financial Futures
on all key terms, persons, places, and concepts.

Online 99 Cents

http://www.epub2174.13.22362.19.cram101.com/

Use www.Cram101.com for all your study needs

including Cram101's online interactive problem solving labs in

chemistry, statistics, mathematics, and more.

20. Financial Planning and Investing in an Efficient Market Context

CHAPTER OUTLINE: KEY TERMS, PEOPLE, PLACES, CONCEPTS

	Asset allocation
	Financial planning
	Diversification
	Systematic risk
	Growth investing

CHAPTER HIGHLIGHTS & NOTES: KEY TERMS, PEOPLE, PLACES, CONCEPTS

Asset allocation	Asset allocation is an investment strategy that attempts to balance risk versus reward by adjusting the percentage of each asset in an investment portfolio according to the investors risk tolerance, goals and investment time frame. Description Many financial experts say that asset allocation is an important factor in determining returns for an investment portfolio. Asset allocation is based on the principle that different assets perform differently in different market and economic conditions.
Financial planning	Financial planning is the task of determining how a business will afford to achieve its strategic goals and objectives. Usually, a company creates a Financial Plan immediately after the vision and objectives have been set. The Financial Plan describes each of the activities, resources, equipment and materials that are needed to achieve these objectives, as well as the timeframes involved.
Diversification	Diversification is a form of corporate strategy for a company. It seeks to increase profitability through greater sales volume obtained from new products and new markets. Diversification can occur either at the business unit level or at the corporate level.
Systematic risk	In finance and economics, systematic risk is vulnerability to events which affect aggregate outcomes such as broad market returns, total economy-wide resource holdings, or aggregate income. In many contexts, events like earthquakes and major weather catastrophes pose aggregate risks-they affect not only the distribution but also the total amount of resources. If every possible outcome of a stochastic economic process is characterized by the same aggregate result (but potentially different distributional outcomes), then the process has no aggregate risk.
Growth investing	Growth investing is a style of investment strategy.

Visit Cram101.com for full Practice Exams

20. Financial Planning and Investing in an Efficient Market Context

CHAPTER HIGHLIGHTS & NOTES: KEY TERMS, PEOPLE, PLACES, CONCEPTS

> Those who follow this style, known as growth investors, invest in companies that exhibit signs of above-average growth, even if the share price appears expensive in terms of metrics such as price-to-earnings or price-to-book ratios. In typical usage, the term 'growth investing' contrasts with the strategy known as value investing.

CHAPTER QUIZ: KEY TERMS, PEOPLE, PLACES, CONCEPTS

1. In finance and economics, _____ is vulnerability to events which affect aggregate outcomes such as broad market returns, total economy-wide resource holdings, or aggregate income. In many contexts, events like earthquakes and major weather catastrophes pose aggregate risks-they affect not only the distribution but also the total amount of resources. If every possible outcome of a stochastic economic process is characterized by the same aggregate result (but potentially different distributional outcomes), then the process has no aggregate risk.

    a. Systematic risk
    b. Systemic risk
    c. Virtual economy
    d. granularity

2. _____ is an investment strategy that attempts to balance risk versus reward by adjusting the percentage of each asset in an investment portfolio according to the investors risk tolerance, goals and investment time frame. Description

    Many financial experts say that _____ is an important factor in determining returns for an investment portfolio. _____ is based on the principle that different assets perform differently in different market and economic conditions.

    a. Asset allocation
    b. Asset location
    c. Assets under management
    d. Eco-investing

3. _____ is a form of corporate strategy for a company. It seeks to increase profitability through greater sales volume obtained from new products and new markets. _____ can occur either at the business unit level or at the corporate level.

    a. Diversity marketing
    b. Figure of merit
    c. Diversification
    d. Global marketing

4. _____ is the task of determining how a business will afford to achieve its strategic goals and objectives.

20. Financial Planning and Investing in an Efficient Market Context

CHAPTER QUIZ: KEY TERMS, PEOPLE, PLACES, CONCEPTS

Usually, a company creates a Financial Plan immediately after the vision and objectives have been set. The Financial Plan describes each of the activities, resources, equipment and materials that are needed to achieve these objectives, as well as the timeframes involved.

a. Flexible product development
b. Float
c. Front-end loading
d. Financial planning

5. _____ is a style of investment strategy. Those who follow this style, known as growth investors, invest in companies that exhibit signs of above-average growth, even if the share price appears expensive in terms of metrics such as price-to-earnings or price-to-book ratios. In typical usage, the term '_____' contrasts with the strategy known as value investing.

a. Guaranteed Investment Certificate
b. Guaranteed investment contract
c. Growth investing
d. Juniperus Capital

Visit Cram101.com for full Practice Exams

Visit Cram101.com for full Practice Exams

ANSWER KEY
20. Financial Planning and Investing in an Efficient Market Context

1. a
2. a
3. c
4. d
5. c

You can take the complete Chapter Practice Test

for 20. Financial Planning and Investing in an Efficient Market Context
on all key terms, persons, places, and concepts.

Online 99 Cents

http://www.epub2174.13.22362.20.cram101.com/

Use www.Cram101.com for all your study needs

including Cram101's online interactive problem solving labs in

chemistry, statistics, mathematics, and more.

Other Cram101 e-Books and Tests

**Want More?
Cram101.com...**

Cram101.com provides the outlines and highlights of your textbooks, just like this e-StudyGuide, but also gives you the **PRACTICE TESTS**, and other exclusive study tools for all of your textbooks.

*Learn More. Just click
http://www.cram101.com/*

Other Cram101 e-Books and Tests

Visit Cram101.com for full Practice Exams

CPSIA information can be obtained at www.ICGtesting.com
Printed in the USA
LVOW03s0850150814

399246LV00002BA/142/P